OVER A BARR

30 YEARS OF LLANRWST CLUB.

MICHAEL JOHN BUCKNALL.

Dedicated to my wife Gill.

Copyright © 2024 Michael John Bucknall.

All rights reserved.

Cover design by: Lucy Jones and Finn Cullimore

Book design by: Lucy Jones and Finn Cullimore

Technical support by: Chloe Jones, Ben Cullimore, and Nathan Bucknall

No part of this book can be reproduced in any form or by written, electronic or mechanical, including photocopying, recording, or by any information retrieval system without written permission in writing by the author.

Published by the Independent Publishing Network

Printed by Book Printing UK www.bookprintinguk.com

Remus House, Coltsfoot Drive, Peterborough, PE2 9BF

Printed in Great Britain

Although every precaution has been taken in the preparation of this book, the publisher and author assume no responsibility for errors or omissions. Neither is any liability assumed for damages resulting from the use of information contained herein.

ISBN 9778-1-8365-436-5-7

Email: pickwicksnwales@aol.com

Facebook: www.facebook.com/michael.bucknall.1949

A CIP catalogue record of this book is available from the British library.

AUTHORS NOTE

The first time I walked into the Royal British Legion, Llanrwst in 1993 something became apparent. It shouted grievances at me, I could see it, smell it and touch it, grievances were unfortunately my "specialist subject".

My last ten years had been a tsunami of grievances, being a trade union official negotiating factory closures across the UK as the country's industrial base shrunk alarmingly.

Gradually against every instinct, I was drawn into another grievance as my new friends entered into a struggle to save their club.

My first impressions were, seeing a bunch of hard drinkin', sweary protesters acting like rebels without a cause.

I could not have been more wrong. Getting to know these "guys", joining them in their justifiable grievance and forging long term friendships with them, has been a privilege and an experience I will always treasure.

The team of " so called dissidents", fully deserve wider recognition for their achievements in the Llanrwst club.

I can only hope this book goes some way to achieving this, on their behalf.

Michael J Bucknall

FORWARD by Jerry Thomas

I have known Mick Bucknall for 30 years, like me he was raised on a Council estate in Bedworth near Coventry,150 miles from my similar experience here in Llanrwst. He is the middle child of five siblings, who left school at 15 to start an apprenticeship in engineering in Coventry. He met Gill when they were both18 years old and were married at 21, buying their first house together in Coventry. (*Sandra and I, like Mick and Gill have been married now for over 50 years)*

By his own admission he was not the greatest of engineers but ruffled a few feathers, when not being paid the full entitlement of wages with his first employer Alfred Herbert's. This dispute was decided in his favour, which culminated in him becoming the youngest *"Freeman of the city of Coventry"* at the time.

Big factories in the midlands had prestigious football teams and great sports facilities. Mick was recruited by Renold Chain Limited, more for his football abilities than his tool making skills, later going on to play and manage the work's football team. We share a love of football, I played and managed teams in and around Llanrwst. Knowing now, what an argumentative sod, he is, it was no surprise he became a shop steward and a year later, the full time union Convener for the factory with 1000 workers, while still in his early twenties. 18 months later he was chairman of the joint negotiating committee covering 12 Renold Chain factories across the UK.

In 1980 the factory where he worked closed, leaving him unemployed. Mick took up a position with the Amalgamated Engineering Union, in their research department, moving Gill and their two young children Jemma and Nathan to Upper Norwood, London. Danielle, their youngest, was born a little later. After a few years, the Electricians union (EETPU) offered him a position in their research department which he took, before quickly being promoted to full time official looking after members in local government and the NHS.

Part of his job was organising annual conferences and being responsible for guests and dignitaries. On one occasion he picked up Dennis Healey, a former Chancellor of the Exchequer

from Blackpool's railway station.
They were walking along the platform when two people shouted *"It's Mike Yarwood"* (Mike Yarwood was an impressionist who was famous for *"taking off"* Dennis on his TV show). Dennis moved his shoulders and large highbrows up and down copying the impressionist's interpretation of him.
In short he saw Dennis Healey taking off Mike Yarwood, doing an impression of himself.
On another occasion the Labour Leader Neil Kinnock arrived late at his hotel along with Charles Clarke (who went on to become Home Secretary). It was late and Charles said to Neil *"Sorry they have just closed the bar"*. Mick's boss said *"Mick you're in charge of guests, sort it out"*. He asked the bar manager for his name. *"Why?"* he asked. *"I need someone to blame when next year's conference is relocated to a more hospitable location."*
Free drinks and apologies quickly followed.
Mick, like me, is proudly working class but has no problem mixing with so-called high fliers. Judge Pickles, a controversial right wing celebrity used to visit Mick's tearoom, specifically to have an argument with him, surprisingly despite their differences, they got on well together and both looked forward to these verbal confrontations.
My favourite *"Mick story"* though is;
A relatively unknown Labour MP, who was a junior minister for employment, arrived to speak at their union conference. Mick had to get him settled in at the hotel and then find a suitable dinner partner for him.
The general secretary and all the union executives were otherwise engaged.
Lord Frank Chapple, Mick's boss said: *"You'll just have to take him to dinner yourself and keep him entertained"*. So they had a meal together and conversed for several hours throughout the evening. Following this, Mick took an interest in his stellar rise through the ranks of the Labour movement, right up to him becoming Tony Blair, Prime Minister in 1997.
Mick also likes to sketch, so I will try to persuade him to include some of his work in his book.

Mick and I first met the day he came to view the Cornucopia Hotel in Llanrwst. He came into the club and I started a conversation with him, mostly talking about football. I thought he was quite young (45 years old) to be giving up the job of a regional union boss based in Southampton. He had been sent there from London, as a trouble shooter to clean up an office with a lousy reputation. Having completed this task successfully over a 5 year period, Mick and Gill sought a new challenge running a business together which brought them to Llanrwst.

Six months later they purchased the rundown property, and changed its name to Pickwick's, both working all hours renovating the building, getting it ready for opening. At the start they did Bed and Breakfast, managed a tearoom in the day and had a restaurant in the evening, employing a chef.

Later they developed the courtyard seating area and excavated a mediaeval well. There came a time when the hotel business no longer interested them, so they retained the tearoom but turned Pickwick's into an antique centre, encompassing a bookshop. These ventures should not be confused with David (grump) Hughes's *"greasy spoon and junk shop which Mick runs"*

Our friendship grew and he became accepted by a wider group inside the club. These new friends had a mix of skills and spent many happy hours in Pickwick's doing jobs while Gill kept us topped up with teas and bacon butties. Mick had joined the Labour party at 16 years of age and been actively involved with them, throughout his trade union career.

He made it very plain his role as an activist was now finished and his family and their new business were his priority now.

Discontent was growing in the club and David Hughes and I were of the view that without changes the club would not survive and It would take a monumental effort to save it. We both saw in Mick someone with the necessary skills to join us and challenge those currently in authority.

We knew Mick was bound to turn us down, which he did, leaving us in no doubt, it would be a battle getting him on board. David and I however can be resolute and resourceful as you will discover and "No" as Mick would say; " *is often negotiable".*

A few of my sketches as requested by Jerry Thomas

Michael Foot Former Labour leader

David "Cookie" Williams Cttee member and vital link between the young and the "coffin dodgers"

Whitby harbour circa 1900

LLANRWST CLUB; OVER A BARREL.

This story is about a group of friends from the Royal British Legion social club in Llanrwst, Conwy, North Wales, who took on the challenge to save their club from imminent closure.
This long tortuous journey by a resourceful, determined group started in the mid 1990s. While writing this account many other RBL clubs have closed, never to reopen again. Sadly many of the characters deserving recognition are no longer with us.
At all levels of the RBL, we met resistance. Instead of recognising us as reformers, we were viewed as "dissidents". Rules were sacrosanct, logic had no place in their world, where the status quo must be preserved at all costs. The club owned by the British Legion, was viewed as a financial asset, by RBL HQ not a community hub serving the people of Llanrwst and the wider Conwy Valley.
We had frustration, disappointment and rejection at every turn. Giving up however, was never an option, we had to succeed both for our dozen employees and the town, which could ill afford to lose this valuable asset. Our opponents, of which there were many, including employed professionals, made a favourable outcome unlikely in this one sided contest. They, however, were hampered by a bureaucratic straight jacket, and an inflexible, soulless *"rulebook"*.
We did have some advantages, while starting out as a ragged outfit, we became a team, developed tactics and more importantly we believed in each other. We shared a sense of humour, which saw us laugh in the face of adversity. Defeats along the way were shrugged off, little victories celebrated;
"Slowly, slowly, catch a monkey" as David Grump would say.
A RBL district official once complained in writing, about a letter we sent, because it highlighted a point in capital letters.
he claimed;
" It *was the equivalent of shouting at him"*.
You would think he had more urgent priorities to deal with.
A slight weakness perhaps, we thought so

*Middle room in 2022, now has a new ceiling
and roof lantern
creating natural light and ventilation.*

*Saturday evening, live football in the middle room, which now
has 4 TV screens. Sometimes there are 4 different programs on
at the same time. If the staff had the wisdom of Soloman, they
would still be unable to settle the arguments, over which
television has the volume switched on.
Having finally resolved this conundrum, someone will no doubt
ask;
"Can I have the JukeBox on?"*

"Winter spring, summer or fall,
all you have to do is call
and I'll be there"
Carol King
"You got a friend."

Chapter 1

Sometime during the summer of 1996, I had a surprise visit from Jerry *"bach"Thomas* and David *"grump"* Hughes, two recent friends of mine. I don't remember the date, but it was a lovely day for sitting in Pickwick's courtyard enjoying a rare day off, listening to the radio. Needing no encouragement to switch off "Barbie girl" which should come with a public health warning.
I asked them,;
"What do *we owe this unexpected pleasure"*
Two hour later, I am trying to take in the magnitude of what was being proposed, because I was genuinely shocked and a little speechless. Not a condition I am noted for, as my friends would testify.
They wanted me to join them in a crusade to democratise the Llanrwst Royal British Legion club, remove the current committee and make it accountable to the membership.
They said;
"We need to arrest further decline and return the club to profitability quickly, or closure will be inevitable"
Asking where I fitted into this plan, as a recent English incomer, who was advised to;
"Keep your head down, avoid any conflicts and try to blend in, as

the best way to get accepted in town".
I saw no reason to deviate from this sensible guidance, which had served me well so far. I thought they were joking,
"It just had to be a wind up".
We all moaned constantly about the club, but then again, we complained about everything: tax, beer prices, Europe, Tories, New Labour, house prices, Brummie visitors, the list is endless. Evenings were incomplete, without a foul mouthed rant about the injustices foisted on us. Dave *"grumps"* rants, were famous and if there was a World Ranting Championship, David would be a worthy Welsh captain. Jerry (bach) then put on his serious head:
"Look, this might be the last chance we have of saving the club, we believe hundreds of people are dissatisfied and could be persuaded to stand alongside us. All three of us have run our own businesses, the club is just another business, being run badly, we could do it better. These guys we're taking on, have never been challenged, we also have the element of surprise in our favour, but we have to strike soon"
"Sorry fellas" I replied
"I have a business to run and haven't got time for this"
Their prime concern was the club's failure to stop money flowing to the landlord, the RBL branch, which is awash with money, while the club is heavily in debt.
David said to me;
"You have plenty of time, you're only running a greasy spoon cafe and flogging a bit of junk, you're not Lovejoy, more like Steptoe, Mick if you ask me"
David needs to stop pussyfooting around and say it as it is. Replying I said;
"Let's assume we come up with a successful plan and the club committee are kicked out or resign en masse. That does not solve the problem, we have to replace them"
Jerry explained, we have thought of that;

"You Mick would be the treasurer, just for a year or so till the finances have been sorted out, We could get Ken Jenkins as Secretary and Edgar Parry as chairman, Colin Owen and big Rich, will be on board, they just don't know it yet "

Under no circumstances was this going to happen, so I replied;

"Treasurer, you're joking, why would I take on this poisoned chalice, I Have no experience of overseeing the financial side of a licenced property and have no desire to do so."

David unrelenting said;

"You're good with figures Mick and a tight arse, that's just what we need"

A backhanded compliment if I ever heard one.

While continuing to protest, I don't ever remember saying "*Yes*", I remember repeatedly saying *"No, No, No"*, on many occasions to no avail, but inexplicably *"maybe"* entered the conversation and without realising it, I became a reluctant participant, finally telling them;

"You better find us a new local, because we are all going to need one soon, when we are all barred for life from the club".

I then impolitely asked them to leave because;

"Steptoe" needed to sort out some junk and get our greasy spoon cafe, ready for tomorrow."

So the madness began or perhaps I should say, the campaign started, with letters to the club committee with a list of grievances.

With no real prospect of success, committing to a plot that will end quickly in defeat, with our opponent damaged, but unbowed, should not be too time consuming.

This is the least you can do for your new friends.

We can then bask in the glory of a battle well fought, lick our wounds and find another boozer.

Just how wrong can you be!

Chapter 2

Three years earlier during the spring of 1993, my wife Gill and I were looking at properties in Wales, having decided to start a business together, for the first time. The Cornucopia Hotel, in Bridge Street, Llanrwst was for sale and we had arranged a viewing whilst staying over in town. We visited the Pen y Bont, run by Ken and Margaret Mayles who were very welcoming and informative about the town.
If we were to buy the property, *"the Bont",* we believed would make a good local. I also visited the Royal British Legion club during the evening.
At the bar Jerry *(bach)*Thomas introduced himself to me.
I remember we spoke about football. He had played for Llanrwst and managed the team in the past, I had done similar, while living in Coventry, playing and managing a factory team.
I was surprised that he and many others followed Liverpool, even more supported Manchester United, given both were 70 miles away across the English border.
Whilst being a long suffering Coventry city supporter, my second team has always been Liverpool so Jerry and I reminisced about their great teams of the past.
Social Clubs in Southampton, where we currently lived, were much cheaper than the pubs. Here, I noticed, there was hardly any difference in price, which was unusual.

Setting up a new business, moving house, uprooting your family and three children, Jemma, Nathan and Danielle was always going to be difficult wherever we moved to.
Schools, doctors, banking and infrastructure were all part of the decision making process, which saw us eventually exchange contracts on October 11th 1993 and become the proud owners of the Cornucopia Hotel.

Had the hotel had a Welsh name, changing it would not be an option, but *"Cornucopia"* Latin for *"horn of plenty"* was not its original name, as it was once the *"Union Tavern"*.
We would never have changed the name from the; *"Union Tavern"*, given my trade union background, but *"Cornucopia"* had no local or historical connection, so it had to go.
As we were both Charles Dickens fans, we opted for; *"Pickwicks Hotel and Tearoom"*, and changed the title deeds accordingly.
The Pen Y Bont did become our local and I also joined the club. Annual subscriptions were £7 to join the Royal British Legion branch. You had to be a member of the RBL branch to join the club, which in 1993 cost a further £2.
Not long after moving, there were redundancies at the Aluminium works, Dolgarrog, and some employees sought advice from me, as it became known that I had been a senior trade union official, prior to moving to Llanrwst.
I had no more answers than the local trade union officers, who had battled tirelessly on behalf of the workers involved.
Closure of the Aluminium works soon followed, a huge loss to the Conwy valley economy.
After some 20 years of negotiating in many industries, the last ten mostly battling against factory closures, I had no ambition to enter local politics or get embroiled in the machinations of any group or organisation. Quite the opposite, Pickwick's and my

family would now take centre stage, with my soapbox and activism retired for good.
We did however give a home to the local Labour party, providing a room and refreshments for their meetings.
Gill reluctantly became the Treasurer, a thankless task given that there was no money to administer, if the truth be known.
Many years ago, aged 23, when working in the tool-room at Renold Chain Coventry, my friend, Roger Mason, without consultation, nominated me as a shop steward. That started a journey to work's convenor, senior negotiator for all Renold Chain sites across the UK, trade union official in London and Area Secretary Southampton, managing 4 officers and staff.
My dear friend Roger still reminds me today, that without him;
"I would have ended up sweeping the factory floor."
My new friend Jerry, like Roger, later developed a plan, unbeknown to me, with consequences lasting three decades.
It's like the line from Hotel California;
"You can check out anytime you like, but you can never leave".
The Llanrwst club has become my;
"but you can never leave", like in the Eagles Classic.
During our first few years, Pickwick's took up all our time, taking on repairs, updating the hotel and tearoom, running an evening restaurant and later developing an antique business.
Regularly moving house, as my union career developed, was very disruptive to family life, with Gill having to sacrifice her career, on several occasions, not to mention the upheaval, foisted on our offspring.
During one move, we left a message for our eldest daughter, Jemma, on her dormitory phone, (no mobile phones then) at Warwick University;
"Don't go home Jemma, you don't live there any more,
Love Mum and Dad. xxx

Chapter 3

Llanrwst Royal British Legion; A brief history.

The building, The Kings Head, Llanrwst is thought to date from the 17th century; Harp maker John Richards was born there in 1711. He was a famous harp maker to Queen Charlotte, wife of King George 111.

The building was sold to its tenant, Mrs Owen for over £1000 in 1891. It was remarked at the time;

"There must be profit in selling drinks to fools".

It is unlikely that enough fools parted with their money, as in 1896 It became "*The Kings Head Temperance Hotel*", owned by the Temperance Society. Many alterations were made to the building at the time, as profits grew. The shareholders enjoyed a 10% annual dividend during its early years, at the peak of the Abstinence Movement.

By 1909 the King's Head was a licensed hotel again, it was also the only property in Llanrwst with a Billiard licence.

Inside the club today is an antique billiard / snooker table by makers E A Clare & Sons. In 1970 the club turned down an offer of £20,000 for the table. There was also interest from Fred Davies, former world snooker and billiards champion, who for a period lived locally in the Conwy valley; his brother Joe won 15 world snooker titles.

A few personal Sketches of Llanrwst circa 1900

The first British Legion Club premises were in Watling street, Llanrwst where a dental practice operates today, moving in just after the war. Military personnel, ex-servicemen and women, made up a significant proportion of the Welsh population at that time.

Between 1949 and 1963 a further 2 million men across the UK aged between 18 and 21 years old were conscripted to National Service. This was a boom time for British Legion Clubs and Llanrwst was no different with an abundance of servicemen applying to join the club. Increased membership meant the club required much larger premises.

They found the ideal solution to this problem, when the club purchased a much bigger property, the Kings Head, Ancaster Square, in 1969, for £5,000 with the help of a Brewery loan. Despite competition from many more public houses than exist today, the club thrived.

The British Legion Club also housed a BL branch with an office situated in the building.

The BL branch is responsible for the welfare side of ex service personnel, including the Poppy Appeal and Armistice. The BL club is a *"not for profit"* company, registered as a friendly society with Companies House. The branch and club attained *"Royal"* status in 1971, it then became the Royal British Legion(RBL).
On November 29th,1973 the club sold the Kings Head to the Llanrwst RBL branch for the grand sum of £5.
Tax advantages are hinted at as a reason for the sale, but really, no one is certain why this transaction took place and it remains a mystery still today.
The Club then signed a 21 year lease to rent the building till 1994.
An agreement was reached that the Club would pay a *"Peppercorn Rent"* of £5 a year.
"Peppercorn rents originated in the 17th century, when a nominal rent was charged on a lease, the lowest coin, a rose bud or a single peppercorn, all items valued at next to nothing"

  The club was now a tenant, but incredibly the agreement made the club responsible for the maintenance, repair and decoration, inside and outside the building. The £5 annual *"peppercorn rent"* did not last long, Rent reviews, well before the 21 year agreement ended, had the club paying hundreds, then thousands a year in rent. Later the branch (landlord) found a more creative way of extracting money, by having the takings from a gaming machine in lieu of rent. There are records showing the gaming machine (bandit) provided £25,000 a year rent to the branch during the 1980s.
The club's grievances over this matter lay unresolved for decades, until a new group of disaffected members joined the fray in the late 1990s.
Yes, that would be us.

Advert for the King's Head

The King's Head, Llanrwst in approximately 1905.
From 1896 the hotel was owned by the Temperance Society at the peak of the abstinence movement. It became an ale house again in 1909 when the "demon drink" became available again, causing great distress to the large "anti drink brigade" and joy to the larger contingent of "drinking men".
Women in Wales weren't allowed in most inns until the 1970s.

"Don't start me talking/
I could talk all night"
Elvis Castello
"Oliver's Army"

Chapter 4

Llanrwst is a rural town, where Welsh is the first language. Sadly, not all of us have the language skills to learn Welsh, but unlike some of my fellow Anglophiles, I like to hear Welsh spoken by my new friends, who are almost all bilingual.

Everyone it seemed had a nickname, David (*grump*) Hughes, a big man like his older brother *(Big Rich)* Richard Hughes, both became close friends. However, anyone listening to our conversations, would think we were sworn enemies, given the insults thrown around.

I don't think I had a compliment from this pair in 25 years, you would be mighty suspicious if you did.

Other new friends were Ken Davies, a decade older,"*Ken 10*", a born storyteller and the Llanrwst RBL standard bearer.

If there was an *"Oscar"* for profanities, Edgar Parry, financial adviser, would be in a "*swear off*" with Big Rich for a place on the Hollywood red carpet. Colin Owen, like most of these characters, is a hard working tradesmen, with a variety of skills. Ken Jenkins local businessman and RBL poppy organiser was also popular amongst this group of friends alongside Ianto Thomas a real local character.

Very often we would play snooker, poorly I might add, with Dave "*grump*" and Jerry "*bach*" pairing off against Edgar and I.

Edgar, I should add; " *is to snooker what Giant Haystacks is to hand gliding, not your ideal partner*". Winning was never an option, what we lacked in talent we made up for in entertainment, with non stop banter and insults traded.

"*Grump*" never had a coin for the lights, it was rumoured he last paid for the light, with an old sixpence, in the pre-decimal era. On those rare occasions when my game improved, with the slim likelihood of a *"break"* occurring, a blow from a cue butt would catch my funny bone, or some other tender region, left exposed whilst bending over a shot.

Despite pleading their innocence, the Hughes brothers were clearly the culprits. Snooker in Wales had become a contact sport, limping home, bruised in some unmentionable places was a common occurrence. It was more dangerous than playing rugby, avoiding injury became the height of my ambition.

It seems I have also acquired a new handle, *"Coventry Mick"*, although this later morphed into *"Mick Pickwick."*

One evening, Jerry *"bach"* said:

"Big Rich had been laid off, without receiving 4 weeks notice, so could I put my trade union hat on, and have a look at this for him"

"Big Rich" really wasn't that bothered, but agreed eventually, I should write to his previous employer. Following my letter, the company agreed, they had been at fault and Rich received the money he was owed. David *"Grumps"* living up to his name said;

"Is that all you got for him" while *"Big Rich"* sort of snarled at me. This is the nearest thing to a thank you, so far from the Hughes Brothers. Big Rich christened the correspondence;

"The dear cxxx letter".

In future years, whether writing to a member regarding discipline, or a supplier not providing a proper service, someone would shout; *"Send them a dear cxxx letter, Mick Pickwick"*

I got to know a few more people, many of them helped with work at Pickwick's, our family home and business, which was a 1598 grade 2 listed building and former coach house.

Bobby Dean, Scouser, affectionately known as "*little Bobby*" was the resident electrician at the club and was a great help with the wiring. Dave *"grump"* did plastering and put a new roof on the garage among other things.

Big Rich and his cousin John Jones built a porch and helped build a laundry room. Jerry *"bach"* was everywhere improving things with his joinery skills. Colin Owen while working in the courtyard discovered a Mediaeval well, which he then helped excavate.

Gill had been talking of having a water feature for sometime, as the courtyard was also a public space where we served food and drinks. The 20 foot deep well met that "*water feature*" requirement perfectly and became a minor tourist attraction once fully restored to its former glory.

Pickwicks Tea Room and Courtyard specialised in Welsh cream teas, with home-made scones, not to be confused with David Grump's "*greasy spoon cafe*"

All this work, but there was never big money charging hands.

In fact the main currency was Gill's famous *"bacon butties"* and a generous number of drinks in the club afterwards.

David *"Grump"* asked if I would represent a member of staff who he believed was wrongly dismissed by the RBL Club committee, a view shared by most of his colleagues.

Reviewing the case, I came to the conclusion;

"The club's officers had not used the procedure properly and risked being taken to a tribunal, unless they reinstated the employee."

At a meeting with the club officers I informed them;

"It could cost the club a lot of money if not resolved locally".

They laughed, saying;

"*The club had no money, so good luck with that".*

I then explained;

"It did not end there, a civil claim could be brought, for damages, against the individuals who authorised the dismissal"

Self preservation then kicked in, at the thought they would personally lose money. Eventually common sense prevailed as

they capitulated and reinstating the employee.
(For the record, the civil claim damages argument was pure fiction, on my part).
The individual whose job was saved, however, was far from happy with my performance, accusing me of being;
"disrespectful and overzealous in my criticism of his employers and friends". Notwithstanding, those so-called "*friends*'" would be further disrespected on numerous occasions by myself and other like minded people in the future, as it turned out.

Around this time, I received the news that my father Ray, had died. All my family still live in and around Bedworth, near Coventry, where I spent my first 21 years. Gill and I have been more nomadic, residing in Coundon, Coventry, Upper Norwood, London, Hayes Bromley, Kent, and West End, Southampton prior to moving to Llanrwst.
We keep in touch with all the family, but are not; "*Just round the corner*" like the rest of my relatives. My mother will be comforted by my sister Christine, brothers, Dennis and Terry and the rest of the Bucknall clan, so she will be in good hands.
It brings back memories of losing my elder brother Jim in 1987 aged 40. Jim was a season ticket holder at Coventry City football club, following them since he was a child. The Sky Blues won the FA cup that year, sadly he never got to see his heroes parade the cup through the streets of Coventry, in a victory celebration, suffering a fatal heart attack earlier that year.
It is irrational but you feel guilty, when you can't instantly join the family to grieve. Feeling somewhat sorry for myself, still early in the day, I went to the club and found a quiet corner, not really seeking company.
After a little while John Jones, Rich and David's cousin joined me and asked;
"if I was okay", sensing something was bothering me.

I opened up about the way I was feeling, which is not the sort of thing blokes do, especially with someone you hardly knew.
We talked for several hours about families and loss.
I cannot recall what John actually said, but have never forgotten the generosity of spirit he displayed that day.
Feeling somewhat better after talking to John I made arrangements to visit the family.
I was called upon to do my fathers eulogy, and was pretty rubbish at it really, considering I used to be paid to address large gatherings as part of my job as a senior Trade Union official.

Jerry *"bach"* on the other hand, is a master at eulogies and I have lost count of the friends I have lost in Llanrwst, where he has blended, a mixture of humour and sympathy, with a skilled delivery at the many funerals I have witnessed.
Jerry is a little bit older than me, so there's a chance he might reach those "pearly gates" before I meet my maker.
I further understand, some of our younger friends, disrespectful as ever, are running a *"book"*, on which of the old guard, Jerry and I *(often referred to as coffin dodgers)* will be, the last one standing, so to speak.
Given his talent for *"farewell funeral speeches"* when my "Grim Reaper" finally arrives Jerry will have to do my eulogy.
I have earned this privilege, but there is a dilemma, I may well outlive him, which means I will be denied, my chosen eulogist.
I do however have a contingency plan, which to date, has not been met with any enthusiasm by Jerry, despite its simplicity, brilliance and originality.
This unique plan is for Jerry to write my eulogy now, not wait till my eventual demise. Maybe run it past me first, so I can correct any parts that show me in a bad light, then record it and put it on a fire stick to be used at my funeral.
Normally circumstances dictate that eulogies are done at short

notice, and invariably these last minute tributes to the recently departed, lack finesse. As I am still alive, when my eulogy is being prepared, the normal time restraints make the process far less time consuming and easier for all concerned.
To paraphrase Boris Johnson;
"He could have a eulogy, oven ready and raring to go".
I know it must be the ultimate in control freakery, to try to influence your eulogist, but I can't resist, so could you also add the following Jerry mate;
"If you live each day as if it was your last, someday you'll most certainly be right " Steve Jobs, Apple.
I would also like;;
"*Baba O'Riley, played by the Who*", really loud.
We don't want people being disrespectful, falling asleep during the proceedings do we.

Jerry and Edgar laying he wreaths for the fallen

On the left, the current Llanrwst club chairman Jerry Thomas, with the former chairman Edgar Parry laying wreaths at
75th anniversary of VE Day. 2020.

Chapter 5

I arrived in Llanrwst as a smoker, a reluctant one, that never smoked in the house, or car, but did enjoy a cigarette with a pint. It was a number of years before the smoking ban applied to pubs and clubs in 2007. Jerry, a fellow smoker, was also a reluctant smoker, who said he was going to give up fags, without resorting to patches or other methods. I doubted he had the willpower, given how addictive nicotine is.
To his credit, several weeks later, he has not succumbed to the dreaded weed and challenged me to do the same.
"Could I match his willpower and give up smoking?"
I was not sure, but nearly 30 years later neither of us have smoked since.
In the club, committee officers are telling women members;
"they can play darts but not use the snooker table",
If this is the policy of the club, I seriously doubt this ruling would survive a discrimination challenge from a female member and will surely be tested in the fullness of time.
During the last five years, conversations, or should I say complaints, were becoming more frequent regarding the running of the branch and the club. Non-service members were by far the largest group of members, easily outnumbering ex-service and women's section members combined
Non-ex service members were classed as *"associate members"* and denied voting rights by the RBL Rules. The largest pool of talent was unrepresented, unable to hold office on the committees or be part of the process for instigating change.
There is a long list of grievances, many dating back decades, including the following;
"Why are minutes of meetings never displayed on the noticeboards.?"

"Why is there a gratuities book behind the bar, for free drinks? Why are the branch officials and selected members receiving free bottles of spirits at Christmas?"

"Why did the Branch run one of the bingo sessions and the Women's section the other, with both organisations profiting from this, at the expense of the club?"

"Why is there no information on income and expenditure available to members?"

"Why is the club paying the branch excessive rent, when the building was given to the branch for nothing years ago?"

"Why, if the branch owns the club, did the club have to pay all running costs, insurance, decorating and maintenance costs?"

"Why is the club £30,000 in debt, allowing the branch,£40,000 in credit, to take £25,000 a year from a gaming machine(bandit).

Nothing sums up the unequal relationship between the branch and the club more than a letter written on 7th May1983.

The club had borrowed money from the bank for essential building work and was struggling financially at the time. It also needed permission from the branch (landlord) for any alterations to the property regardless how minor they may be.

The Honorary branch secretary wrote to the Club chairman;

"Dear Sir

At a meeting of the Llanrwst British Legion Branch Executive Committee held on the 3rd May 1983 permission was granted to the RBL Club Llanrwst to carry out alterations and extensions to the Branch premises of which the RBL Club are our tenants. But it must be understood that the Branch landlords will in no way be financially involved in the above works, but, as always we will be at hand."

A shorthand version could easily read;

"The Branch own the building, the club repair, maintain and insure it, but don't you dare do anything without our permission, we will be watching you, and will not be paying for anything"

Chapter 6

Back in the club, members are angry, beer prices are going up again, membership is falling, there are real fears that the club could be closing, information about the state of the club is sparse, so rumours were rife. The beer is currently the same price as the pubs, within a few pence, and further price increases could be avoided, if the rent was cheaper.

A few ex- service members, Edgar Parry, Ken Jenkins, Ken Davies and Bobby Dean had joined the committees on occasions hoping to gain information and hopefully bring changes to the running of the club. The problem was the branch was the dominating group, strongly supported by the women's section, so their influence was limited.

The main area of concern was the club had a gaming machine (bandit) and the branch had the takings of the second bandit, therefore denying the club thousands of pounds of income.

Edgar Parry asked if he could be present when they counted the takings. They told him;

"Okay be there tomorrow at 9.00 am when the machine will be emptied".

He duly arrived early at 8.45, to be informed;

"He was too late, it had already been done."

The message was quite clear;

"Mind your own business, stay out of things that don't concern you", an attitude that would continue as more questions got asked.

It has been at least 5 years since there was an AGM for the Branch, Club or Women's section.

It was understood that each of these different groups kept handwritten records of their meetings, but there was no apparent requirement to publish this information to members.

Members frustrated by the lack of transparency, requested a

compromise whereby;
"All key decisions, to be displayed on the noticeboards"
This compromise failed to find favour with the officers of the various committees. Similar suggestions for better communications were also rejected.

During the summer of 1996, there was a heated discussion going on, in the bar about the "*branch hospitality book*", that's kept behind the bar. It seems that certain branch officers would have free drinks for themselves, colleagues and friends.
These drinks would be recorded in the "*hospitality book*" and at the end of the year the club would be reimbursed by the branch for the free drinks. This was not a new practice, it had in fact, gone on for many years.
Records which do exist are ambiguous, referring to *"miscellaneous sundries"* and "*entertainment costs unspecified*". However, in surviving handwritten minutes from January 1982, there was an attachment from the hospitality book which confirmed;
"The *branch paid the club £1075 for drinks"*
You could purchase 1,791 pints at 60p for £1075 in 1982.
At today's prices (£2.50 a pint in 2024) that is the equivalent of spending £4477 on free drinks for committee officers and their cronies.
The discussion at the bar continued, with reference to Christmas gifts, which consisted of free bottles of spirits for selected committee members. Several said they had seen; *"officers, with their arms full of bottles, leaving the club around Xmas time"*.
The branch was allegedly paying the club the cost price of the spirits, so the club was not out of pocket with these arrangements.
 The late Peter (Cockney) a local plumber said;
"*While working at a prominent branch members house, who will*

remain anonymous, there were so many bottles behind the sofa, a mishap with his welder could have blown up half the town"
The Women's section also came in for criticism, for having a *"Jolly"* to the Royal Welsh Show each year, *"under the pretext of recruitment."* It was pointed out that their only income came from raffles and bingo held in the club.

Some disaffected members of the women's section had started to ask questions, regarding elections, frequency of meeting, the non-publishing of accounts and the lack of any information, on their under used noticeboard.

Their reward for such insolence was being labelled *"trouble makers"*, ignored and sidelined.

Complaints about the plight of associate members (non ex Service) were common, in a system stacked against them. Could they be mobilised into something more than a *"talking shop"*, most people doubted it.

Service personnel, coming back from World War 2, or later, from National Service, joined British Legion clubs in massive numbers.. There was no need to consider the plight of a tiny group of non-service *"associate members"*, as this group would have been insignificant. They could join other working men's clubs or other similar organisations, if unhappy with their status in the RBL..

No one could have predicted that 50 years later, this little group of non-service members would make up the majority of the membership of British Legion clubs, with ex-service personnel now being a small and ageing minority

As National service ended in 1963, the rules effectively reduced the pool of talent able to serve on RBL committees to those born before 1945, unless they came from a professional military background.

The Armed Services have been declining as a proportion of the

population year on year, this fact however was seemingly overlooked until 2003, when a new rule democratising representation to every member was introduced.
Sadly it came too late for most British Legion clubs and failed to stop the rate of club closures across the whole of Wales.

The club's financial woes stem from a massive increase on the £5 annual peppercorn rent, paid to the branch in the early 1970s to £13,000 in the early 1980's Not satisfied with that, later in August 1989 at the monthly branch meeting, the following resolution was carried;

"It was proposed that the Branch take full (control) of the bandit, from the club, including taking over the keys from the club. They (The branch) would empty the cash out, each Monday"

This resulted in the branch having the takings from the bandit in lieu of rent, meaning the club's rent went up from £15,600 to £25,000 a year.

Who gave the branch the authority to control the club affairs so undemocratically and undermine the already fragile club finances?

Why the club agreed to this humiliation, is unknown as club minutes of the meetings for the period have conveniently disappeared?

Unlike the club, the branch is not a business, so it cannot have a licence for a gaming machine, by the same token it cannot rent a gaming machine and is not VAT registered.

The *"reformers"* brought this moral and illegal practice to the attention of RBL officials and were told;

"What the branch do is none of our business".

*"As the present now
will later be past
The order is rapidly fadin'*
Bob Dylan
"The times they are a changin'

Chapter 7

There was obviously a time when the RBL club and RBL branch worked in harmony providing comradeship and benevolence to the community facing hardship, during difficult times especially after the war. This is apparent in the few old handwritten minutes from the 1950s.

We have a record of attendance for a Llanrwst branch meeting, which had Lord Aberconway, 2 MPs, an Army Chaplain and other senior officers in attendance, demonstrating how important the organisation was in the past.

They had a hardship fund, which war widows and the poor in the community benefited from.

The club with limited democratic powers and declining economic opportunity, has seen this harmony and comradeship disappear with the branch/ landlord prospering, while the club continues its downward trajectory.

While the branch was considered the real obstacle to change, by many, the women's section was not immune from criticism, being similar to the branch with regards to secrecy, and subservient to the branch officers in all matters

While this barroom debate raged on between members, about the blatant inequality between the different sections of membership, a prominent women's section member was seen entering a door marked *"private"* and coming out with her glass

topped up with a short.
Having witnessed this occurrence several times, someone naively asked,
"If there was another secret bar, through the door marked private".
They were told;
"A visit to the secret stash was a regular occurrence, this person and others never seemed to pay for drinks like the rest of us".
The obvious question was;
Why are there so many grievances and why is nothing being done to resolve them?
"We are second class members and fancy titles like associate member, don't disguise that fact. What's the use of attending a branch AGM if you are not allowed to speak or vote?"
was a constant refrain, as was;
" Things will never change"
It was joked;
"The branch ran courses in secrecy for the local Masonic lodge"

Researching this book, we did discover a few rumblings of discontent during the early 1980s. One committee member stated;
"The branch should give more help to the club from its funds"
He was told in no uncertain terms;
"It was a stupid suggestion".
This may not have been the most subtle reply, but that seemed to end the matter.
On another occasion at an AGM in the late 1980s, questions were asked about the club's finances. A member was not satisfied with the reply and demanded more information.
The chairman refused to answer the questions, closed the AGM and called a committee meeting to discuss matters in private.

Things have not progressed at all over the years and openness is a concept, beyond their comprehension still.

With a turnover of £200,000 in 1996, the two biggest items of expenditure for the club are wages and stock from the brewery. Together they make up more than 80% of the club's total expenditure, both costing around £90,000 each. With most hospitality workers, including bar staff on National Minimum Rates (NMR) It's difficult to reduce this liability, other than cutting staff, or reducing hours.
Nothing suggests these two factors were the problem then, any more than they are today.
There are marginal savings, to be made with the remaining 20% overheads, but realistically, the cost of stock provides the biggest opportunity to get the club's cost under control, in conjunction with, taking the gaming machine back from the branch to the club.
The price of stock, wet sales, is influenced by your bargaining power. A club with no brewery loans can have multiple suppliers, breweries aren't keen on these and will offer a better deal to be the sole supplier. They will also want a longer agreement, which guarantees them selling exclusively to you, over a greater period, this also comes at a price.
Most breweries would prefer customers to have loans with them, indefinitely, knowing one's ability to influence the price of stock is negligible until the loan is eventually paid off .
It's difficult to imagine a worse set of circumstances in which to trade, than those faced by Llanrwst RBL club. It is not competitive on price with the neighbouring pubs, bearing in mind, you don't need a membership card to buy a pint in your local pub.
Why join the club, paying around £10 membership for the privilege, only to pay roughly the same price for your drinks.

The club televisions are ancient, no different to what you have in your house, mounted on the walls. The televisions were as deep as they were high, weighing nearly a hundredweight each. No sensible member would ever walk under them, for fear of being crushed to death, if they did.

Facilities overall were no better than the pubs, with one exception, the club does have a concert room which provides entertainment, which was especially popular before the millennium, particularly at weekends, during bank holidays and on festive occasions.

To sum up, the club has a greedy landlord completely unsympathetic to its tenants difficulties, an unfavourable brewery agreement, poor facilities and falling membership.

Big Rich summed it up succinctly;

"The brewery had the club over a xxxxxxx barrel"

and the branch had:

"The club, in its xxxxxxx pocket and over a xxxxxxx barrel"

On Armistice Sunday 1997, following a service at St Grwst church, the procession from Ancaster square, Llanrwst, led by Ken Davies, The Royal British Legion, Standard Bearer, begins its march to the Cenotaph 400 metres away.

There are 200 people assembled at the cenotaph, for the service in Welsh and English. 24 Wreaths are laid by individuals and organisations. For more than 50 years Edgar Parry has laid a wreath for his father, who died during the last day of the war in 1945, weeks before he was born

The crowd having paid their respects to the fallen, make their way to the RBL club, where a buffet for 150 is waiting for them with tea and coffees. For those wishing for something stronger, the bars are open, where the staff dressed solemnly for the occasion are waiting to welcome them.

After the Buffet, Ted, Jerry's brother, a Manchester City fan, is

winding up United fans in the snooker room, who are holding up two fingers mockingly reminding him Manchester United are still premiership champions. Ken Jenkins quite rightly takes the plaudits along with Ken Davies for another successful Poppy Appeal and the smooth organisation of today's event. Very few people realise how much work goes into this annual event;
There are flowers for the church.
Liaison with the vicar, so the service ends precisely on time, prior to them assembling on the square.
Close cooperation with the police, who close off several roads so the procession can complete its journey to the Cenotaph.
Club staff assemble the trestle tables, prepare the conference room and make 100 or so teas and organise refreshments for the children attending.
The sound system for the event needs setting up and the bugler has to be booked for *"the last post"*.
Locally made fresh sandwiches and cakes require a 5.00 AM start for caterers to meet the tight deadlines for delivery by 11.30 am.
Earlier in the week, Jerry, David and Ted clean in and around the Cenotaph, repaint where necessary, check the flagpoles, replace flags and generally have everything looking pristine, for that special occasion each year, when it takes centre stage.
There was quite rightly justified criticism of many of the branch activities, but they could not be faulted for the way the Poppy appeal and Armistice was organised which everyone in town was proud of.
The branch was coming under pressure, for the thousands it spent each year from the proceeds of the gaming machine.
The branch knew as a registered charity, it was not allowed to give any of the membership concessions or gifts, as this conflicted with the rules of the RBL Royal Charter.
Branch secretaries were told by their respective RBL district

officers, to send any surplus over £1000 to them or transfer it into their COIF charity fund, which is controlled centrally. The branch had 40 times this amount in its funds (*all from their gaming machine*) and showed no inclination to follow RBL national policy. Its accounts show it once had £69,000 at its disposal.

There was good news however, in August 1998 the club sold "*The Star*" a neighbouring property, it purchased as an investment in the early 1990s, after much pressure from members to clear their debts. Retaining the car park and ownership of the access, at the side of the building, between "*the Star*" and the "*Kings Head,*" meant the club now owned the car park, while the branch owned the club.
The new owners of The Star *"have the benefit of a right of way in the car park."*
All buildings owned by the RBL are covered by an insurance policy nationally, with the club paying the premiums. This arrangement makes the tenant pay rather than the landlord. This adds insult to injury when you consider all building and maintenance of the property are also the clubs responsibility. Should the club wish to purchase the property in the future, the price could be inflated by improvements the club makes to the infrastructure. There is therefore a disincentive for the club to spend money on upgrading the Kings Head.
The club separately arrange their own policy for fixtures and fittings, along with public indemnity.

Former world darts champion Bob Anderson, (arms folded) praised the darts facilities during a recent visit to the the club

Chapter 8

Following further Pickwick's courtyard meetings, the reformers got to work. The club committee agreed to talks with disaffected club members, Jerry, David and Edgar, to foster better relations. I was *"persona non grata"*, accused by senior branch officers of trying to close the club down, to form a Labour club, so was conspicuous by my absence.

The reformers, "dissidents" as we were referred to in earlier correspondence, were invited to a meeting of the club committee, and surprisingly minutes were produced.

They stated that; *"Progress was being made slowly but surely"*, Sadly that's not true..

Extract from May 4th 1999 branch minutes

"A lengthy discussion ensued during which many questions were asked on both sides. A wealth of information was disclosed by the three members and the committee, resulting in the air being cleared.

The members were thanked for their time and interest in club affairs. A collective letter, one of which was sent to Mr Bucknall, contained a number of charges which in his case, proved to be unfounded. All charges have been withdrawn and the secretary instructed to write to this effect together with an apology for any distress caused."

It is not unusual when reading these minutes to;

"lose the will to live".

The *"reformers"* did not waffle these platitudes as published in the minutes, but stated precisely and unambiguously what they wanted the branch committee to do.

That is; *"Return the bandit to the club, lower the rent and reduce prices, with a better deal from the brewery.*

This dispute will escalate without major reforms as the club will be uneconomic and eventually close."

It insults our intelligence, when you paraphrase the" *"reformers"* comments with such nonsense, replacing their words with bland non statements such as;
""A lengthy discussion," "a wealth of information" "the air being cleared"
It appears the minute secretary of the meeting, has turned into (Jim Hacker from Yes Minister) and continued his linguistic patter when referring to me;
"the case was proved to be unfounded"
A club official had attributed remarks to me, which were untrue;
"Mr Bucknall wants the RBL turned into a Labour Club".
This was a lie, it is not *"unfounded"* as the minutes state, and the official making this accusation should be made to resign, as he is unfit to hold any office in the RBL.
This blatant lie was designed to undermine my credentials and silence me, which it did successfully on this occasion, by vetoing my attendance at the meeting.
Following the meeting David (*grump*) saw it as a weakness on their part, trying to bar my attendance and said:
"Last time you met them, resulted in the successful reinstatement of an employee they had sacked. The bxxxxxxxs are hardly going to welcome you with open arms after that, so you should take it as a compliment. Authority is slowly draining away from them and their desperation is beginning to show."
Despite the correlation with Jim Hacker, there is a serious message.
The meeting never acknowledged any grievance and is not open to change. We have to find ways to make them change, or replace them.
David and Jerry are becoming regular visitors to Pickwick's as the campaign gains momentum. We are also critical of the club committee's dealings with the brewery who raised beer prices without any consultation.

According to the club minutes;
"Prices were fixed as low as possible"
This gives the false impression that they have some influence on this, which is clearly not the case.

Our expected expulsion from membership of the RBL seems less likely since we last met, but we must not become complacent.
Gill is already finding decorating and repair jobs for me, anticipating my expulsion, and Jerry's wife Sandra and daughter Linsey are making similar plans.
This dispute could get very dirty, with truth already a casualty, when trying to undermine us. We should expect more of the same, when it dawns on them;
" We are not going away"
Both Jerry and David think that there are cracks beginning to show in the unity of the club committee, therefore it's important we keep the pressure on.
We expect concessions to be made at the next unofficial meeting to ward off a wider rebellion.
The objections to me attending meetings were withdrawn, but it was decided that Edgar, David and Jerry continue with the consultation while I concentrate on correspondence with the RBL district officers to further the *"reform"* case.
One of my accusers, a senior officer from the club committee, confronted me one evening, pleading his innocence, regarding remarks about me. Being far from convinced by his sincerity, I responded;
"I'll make a deal with you, you stop telling lies about me and I'll stop telling the truth about you"

.

Chapter 9

There are leaks coming out of the branch, that they are considering returning the gaming machine back to the club, *in exchange for £15,000 a year.* Currently the branch has total control of the keys and are taking approximately £25,000 or more from the bandit annually. £10,000 off the rent is a good start, the equivalent of 10p off a pint in 1996/97.
There are further reports that many members of the club committee are considering retiring, having served the club for many years. Most were not heavily involved in the decision making process. They now find, their misplaced loyalty, makes them unjustly associated with alleged mismanagement.
We had some sympathy with this position, as collateral damage was inevitable.
David said;
"There were existing committee members, we could work with, they included Victor Thomas and Harold Sinkinson".
Support from the district office regarding spending charitable money on coach trips and Xmas gifts was falling away and the branch committee in a last desperate move, asked advice from their solicitors;
"Are these Xmas payments to members a breach of the rules with regards, to the RBL Royal Charter?".
Instead of stating the obvious, the branch received woolly advice from the solicitors about renaming the payments;
"seasonal supplements instead of xmas gifts"
To think they were paying for this; *"Mickey Mouse legal advice"* with member's money, was incredulous.
The realisation must have hit home, that their position was becoming more and more untenable.
We discussed what options the current club committee had, before coming to the conclusion, they were probably consulting

the rulebook, to see what disciplinary powers could be used against us,other than expulsion, in a last desperate attempt to keep control of the club.
David said;
"You're the rules man Pickwick, with your union background, get you arse in gear, find something in the rules that benefits us".
I agreed to study the rules with the forlorn hope;
"Something will turn up" As Wilkins Micawber famously said in David Copperfield.
The pressure on the branch committee as well as the club committee was intensifying. By challenging their right to spend money contrary to the RBL rules, we successfully curtailed their costly vanity projects. It further weakened the argument for retaining the gaming machine money, as they could not justify spending the money they received from it.
It was no surprise therefore, when posters from the branch secretary were circulated around the club and on the notice boards

IT IS WITH REGRET THAT THE BRANCH COMMITTEE WILL NOT BE IN A POSITION TO MAKE ANY DONATIONS OR PAYMENTS OF ANY DESCRIPTION (INCLUDING THE A.O.P. CHRISTMAS GIFTS) FROM ITS FUNDS FOR THE FORESEEABLE FUTURE.

There was a concerted effort, to blame the loss of these benefits onto the *"reform group"*, despite our clear position,that any new club committee elected, would take responsibility for maintaining these payments, when setting up a new club benevolent fund unfettered by RBL rules and charter restrictions that apply to the branch.

> *"Every generation blames the one before,*
> *and all of their frustrations,*
> *come beating on your door"*
> Mike and the Mechanics
> *"The living years"*

Chapter 10

Reading the club rules did, after all, provide an unexpected opportunity for us, so it was decided we would demand a Special General Meeting (SGM) under rule 16.3.

"A SGM shall be called by the club secretary in the following circumstances;

(a) on a requisition, signed by one fifth of the financial members or

(b) thirty such members whichever is the least, stating the proposed special resolution thereof the requisition must include both the printed name and signature of the members".

There are further clauses covering notice boards and advertisements in the local paper. It should be noted only ex service members (*financial Members*) could sign a petition. This meant the majority of non service members (*associate members*) were excluded from this process.

Rule 20 Removal from office.

"The Committee or any member or members thereof, including the elected officers may be removed by the votes of the two thirds of the members present and voting at a SGM called for that purpose".

There were several hundred members prepared to sign a petition, but most were "*auxiliary members*", who had no voting rights and could not sign a petition. Despite this setback, we had no problem getting 30 ex-service members to sign a petition and on completion of the paperwork, David Hughes wrote to the Club secretary with the following proposition.

"This special General meeting has no confidence in the club committee and demands their removal"
On receiving the petition, the committee chairman took advice from the district officials in Wrexham on the legitimacy of the action, as no one had any experience in this type of challenge. They were informed the petition complied fully with the RBL rules and a Special General Meeting (SGM) must be called as soon as possible.
It must have been a shock to the district officers, that growing discontent had fuelled such an extreme reaction, to the current Llanrwst RBL committee.

A Special General Meeting was called for June 14, 1999.
There was a huge turn out, the conference room seats were full, with others standing at the back and sides with approximately 150 members in attendance. The chairman opened the meeting, clearly surprised at the turnout and read out the proposition which David Hughes had sent demanding the removal of the existing committee.
He explained if the motion was passed, a new set of elections would have to take place and outlined the time scale involved. Members wanted to know why there had not been an Annual General meeting for a while and criticised the lack of information and secrecy regarding the clubs finances.
Alex King, the owner of the "*Victoria Inn*" tried to get a point across, but was told to:
"Sit down and stop being a troublemaker".
Alex, refusing to be cowered by the chairman, replied in a booming cockney accent, reminiscent of Alf Garnett;
"Don't you tell me what I am, I'll tell you what you are, your a tosser a Fxxxxxx tosser, that's what you are."
The room erupted in applause with the chairman completely flustered, having lost all authority. The chairman ploughed on

hardly making any defence to the criticism directed at the existing committee, before finally putting the resolution to the meeting.

The vote for the resolution was overwhelming, which meant the club committee was removed from office.

New elections would follow, organised by the departing club officials

The mood in the club afterwards was celebratory, resulting in some very sore heads the next morning.

What started with three people, with no voting rights, had successfully overcome its first hurdle. Three years of campaigning and momentum was shifting in our favour, but we must not become complacent..

If we make a mistake now and fail to win the elections, everything will have been in vain.

There is still much work to be done in the next few weeks to mobilise support and we must leave nothing to chance.

Finding a quiet corner towards the end of the evening, David reminded Jerry and I;

" *If we don't win this forthcoming election, we really will need to find a new boozer, because we will never be forgiven*"

Jerry said;

"*Dave and I might need a new pub, but you Mick Pickwick will probably get run out of town*"

On that happy note the evening ended.

"Power tends to corrupt; absolute power corrupts absolutely."

An observation Lord Acton made in a letter to Bishop Creighton on April 5th 1887

What lengths would certain individuals in the Llanrwst club go to hold onto power?

"We were about to find out, in the most dramatic of circumstances"

Women getting into the spirit of VJ Day 2005

Dressed in uniforms from the 1940s, These volunteers helped feed over 150 pensioners on Llanrwst Square and brought a party atmosphere to the celebrations both outside and later inside the club, where live music continued well into the evening.

VJ Day on the square and in the club later

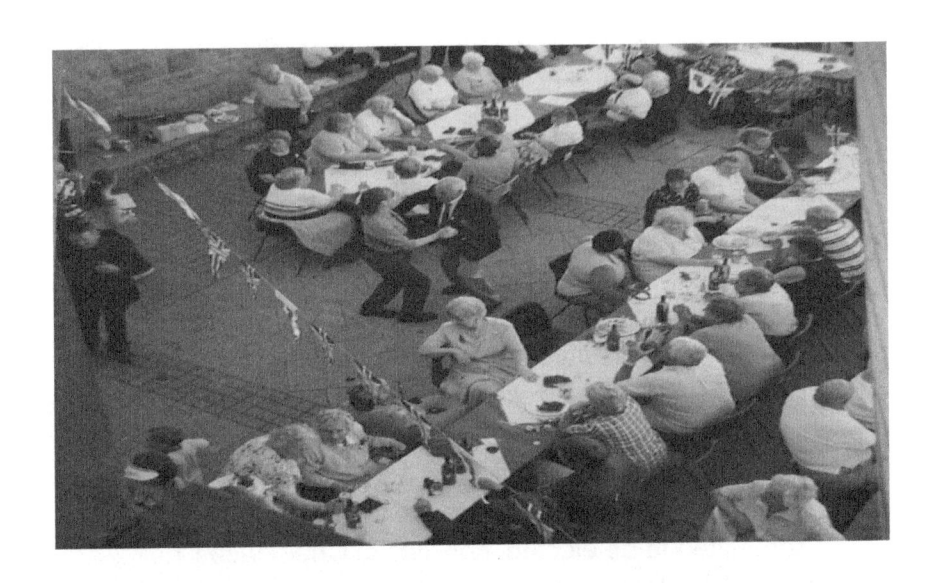

Chapter 11

On the 6th July 1999 the Llanrwst Club secretary received the petition and agreed to send a letter, giving details of the election, to every member in the postal district, the whole process would be completed in 9 days.
12th,13th,14th July --Nominations for election
15th, 16th,17th, July------ Election voting dates
18th July-------counting of vote
20th July ------ meet to declare results
There is a room to the left of the club entrance, which the doorman uses as his office. This had a hatch with a letterbox and during the forthcoming election completed ballot papers would be posted through the letterbox, for counting at a later date.
The doorman vacated the office for the duration of the election, and assurances were given, as to the security of this process.
The committee to be elected, consists of Chair, Vice Chair, President, Vice President plus eight committee members.
The Secretary and Treasurer are appointed by the committee.
The nomination sheets were posted.
Those nominated in opposition to *"the reformers"* included three complete strangers, along with nine others, who were mostly supporters of the retiring club committee officers.
With over one hundred turning up at the SGM, mostly supporting "The reformers", hopes were high that the "*slate*" containing Edgar, Jerry, David and 8 others would get elected.

On the 20th July 1999 there was a large turnout in the club, almost all being reform supporters, waiting for the declaration. The result, when announced, was an annihilation for the "*reformers*", with none of our "*slate*" being elected.
Every supporter of the "*old guard*" including the three complete

strangers were all declared winners, by the broadly smiling, former chairman..

We had defeated the old committee, forcing them to resign, but their proxies had won every single officer and committee position. *"It was an unmitigated disaster"*.

Three years of campaigning had culminated in a humiliating defeat. I could hardly look David and Jerry in the face.

How would they cope with such a disappointment, after investing so much of their time, energy and commitment into this project..

Then something strange started to happen, it started as a murmur before increasing in intensity. The crowd were angry and were voicing their concerns. Suspicion was rife that foul play was involved, a view not shared, by a small number of the women's section committee members, branch officials, or a coterie of former club committee officers, enjoying the "dissidents" humiliation.

Their celebrations were short lived, as the deception and subterfuge unravelled at breathtaking speed.

Questions rained on those who conducted the ballot.

Bobby Dean angrily accused the organisers of;

"Conducting a fraudulent election"

Other members joined in seeking further explanations;

"They asked for a breakdown of the voting figures?"
"How many ballot papers were issued?"
"How many had voted?"
"Who counted the vote?"
"Was the vote overseen by scrutineers?"
" How many votes did each candidate receive?"

There were further demands to see;

"the actual completed ballot papers".

The Chairman assured everyone that;

"Election rules had been properly observed and took exception to

suggestions of impropriety."

In reply to the specific questions raised by the members the chairman said;

"*They did not know how many ballot papers were issued, or the numbers voting. They could not provide us with the completed ballot papers, as they had gone missing. They had no figures for each candidate and were not prepared to tell us, the person or persons who counted the vote, claiming bizarrely, it was a secret ballot, so they could not reveal this information*".

Failure to even explain the irregularities or answer further questions was not well received. Further procrastination followed, then an attempt to close the meeting early, inflamed the situation further.

Those in attendance were furious and refused to accept that the vote had not been rigged. Even those enjoying our humiliation earlier, seemed embarrassed by the inept and ham-fisted attempt to stop the "*reform candidates*" being elected.

There was talk about bringing RBL Officials to Llanrwst to hold an investigation. In normal circumstances, this would have been appropriate, but this would take time, perhaps months to resolve. We did not have the luxury of time, there was only a narrow window of opportunity for us and the clock was ticking on how long the club could survive.

It was agreed by those attending the declaration meeting, that a secret ballot rerun be held, with the same nominations on the ballot papers.

Independent scrutineers were elected to oversee the election which would be held ASAP.

David Hughes pledged;

"*He would get a General Election Ballot box with security tags, from his contacts, within the County Council, so that the next election would be totally democratic*".

The Ballot Box would remain on the bar for the duration of the election.

The result would be displayed on the notice boards and include the votes cast and votes each candidate received.

David did get his secure ballot box from the council and the new election took place.

Jerry and David were confident that *"the reformers"* would win most of the seats contested in the election, while I was less than convinced about the outcome.

Three days later on the 23rd July 1999, the ballot box was opened and the votes counted, overseen by elected scrutineers. The election result was declared to a smaller audience, with very few of the opposition in attendance, perhaps the voters were suffering from *"election overload"*.

The result was a complete reversal of the bogus election, with reform candidates winning every position.

The following people being elected;

President Mr A King, Vice President Mr K Davies, Chairman Mr E Parry, Vice Chair Mr D Hughes, Mr J Thomas, Ms S Thompson, Mr H Sinkinson, Mr D Clift, Mrs A Pritchard, Mr R Hughes. Mr C Owen.

No one questioned the validity of the new election, despite all the previous winners becoming defeated candidates in the new election. It was fair and importantly seen to be fair.

The election of a new committee may not be welcomed by the district RBL but the result is unlikely to be challenged.

The Llanrwst RBL branch is still the dominant power and club landlord, so while these club elections are significant, they are not in themselves game changing.

For the club to survive and prosper the financial restraints imposed by the branch will have to change. Hopefully the branch will recognise this, because without reform the club's position becomes more critical as each day passes

> *"I did my best to notice*
> *when the call came down the line"*
> The Killers
> "Human"

Chapter 12

Prior to calling the first meeting of the new RBL Club Committee, David, Jerry and I assembled in the lounge at Pickwick's, for a debrief. There was no jubilation, no fist pumps, the last few weeks had been draining for all of us.

As we talked, the realisation of the task ahead seemed overwhelming. We had gone from *"dissidents'* and *"reformers",* to employers today, with a duty of care to all the staff and members..

Not all the staff welcomed the new committee, as we were an unknown quantity.

The rules do not allow employees to participate in elections, so they had little choice in the matter of who their new bosses would be. We made the meeting of staff our first priority, officers would meet them in the next few days, to give assurances about their future employment.

With the club finances looking so bad, the worst case scenario was, the club closing in the immediate future, worst still, it could happen on our watch, with that being our lasting legacy.

Arguing we had inherited a catastrophic situation, would not wash with the membership, when looking for someone to blame. This was going to be a stressful brief with the committee looking at us to provide leadership.

The inaugural club committee meeting took place on the 3rd August 1999. Harold Sinkinson from the previous committee was given a special welcome, having supported reform against the former regime.

Ken Jenkins was appointed secretary, with myself appointed treasurer. A condition of accepting the treasurer's job was that I did not handle the cash, which was too time consuming, given my own business demands. Sheila Thompson, David Hughes's partner, agreed to be vice treasurer and count the money.

Gone was the secrecy that had pervaded the club for so long, we would meet monthly, publish the minutes of every meeting on the noticeboards. A financial statement of income and expenditure, would be included in the minutes, along with up to date membership figures and stocktake reports every month. Annual General Meetings (AGM's) would be strictly adhered to and any member could inspect the club's books, after giving a week's notice.

Committee members would serve for two years, but to keep some continuity, half the committee would be subjected to election each year. With so many issues requiring attention, a financial sub committee was formed to examine every item of expenditure and seek negotiations with all the suppliers, utilities, branch landlord and bank to cut the expenditure of the club. Jerry Thomas, David Hughes and myself were trusted with the responsibility of being the financial sub committee.

Alex King, our brave and outspoken friend died, before taking up the presidency, his widow, Kay took on the mantle serving with distinction for a number of years, before being replaced as president by Ken Davies.

Within days, the finance sub committee met the club's bank manager, the purpose being to secure a business loan, to tide the club over, for the next few months
There was a list of prerequisites needed to qualify for a loan, ten in fact, if my memory serves me right. He pompously talked of the need for *"due diligence"* like a headmaster addressing school children;
"Did you make a profit last year?"
"Did sales increase last year?"
"Have you ever run a licensed property before?"
"Do you expect to pay off the brewery loan soon? "
After six more questions, all answered in the negative, the bank manager's demeanour went from mild frown to deep grimace, as he delivered his considered reply.
His words are still lodged in our collective brains a quarter of a century later;
"The business is not a viable proposition, therefore the bank could not invest in such a risky venture"

If the bank is right, the prospect of turning things around, will be an enormous task, with the odds firmly stacked against us.
"How did I let myself get involved in this, when it's been difficult enough running our own fledgling business, Pickwicks, without having the stress associated with the club's financial difficulties?.
This bank manager appraisal, seemed to to concur with Big Rich's view of the situation, while adding *"the bank"* to our current woes;
"The brewery and bank had the club over a xxxxxxx barrel" and the branch had:
"The club, in its xxxxxxx pocket and over a xxxxxxx barrel"

Staff and committee members old and new, with some well known characters and the odd rogue . Left to right;
Stan, Sheila, Colin, Neil, Wayne, Jackie, Paul, Steve, Michael, Anne, Julie, Cath, Rob, Debbie, Mennigs and Miriam.

Chapter 13

We closed the business bank account, and opened a new one with a different bank, calling it *"a new business"* therefore receiving 18 months free banking, saving approximately £4500. In1999 everyone paid cash for drinks in the club, staff were paid in cash and most bills were paid by cheque.

You paid to put cash in the bank and paid to take cash out, It was a costly business. I did not envy Sheila having to count it all.

Next we set up a meeting with a rival brewery, our current supplier was oblivious to this and over a few days, put a deal together.

Negotiations centred around the volume of sales (barrelage). We convinced our prospective brewery that our club membership would grow, leading to an increase in barrelage of 25%.

They agreed incremental discounts based on volumes.

With the prospect of almost £100,000 worth of new business a year, they were keen to win our account. Their original pitch was far removed from their final improved offer, which is a vast improvement on our existing deal, even if our sale volumes remained the same.

Part of their sales pitch was to take the whole committee to one of the pubs, the brewery supplies, to try out their beers, whilst attempting to convince us what good partners they could be.

We came to the conclusion, we could save a considerable amount of money and the members would get used to the different beers.

There were a few unconvinced by this, preferring the beer we had, if not the price.

A deadline for signing contracts was agreed, some three weeks ahead. The talks with our potential new supplier were in fact a

"*trial run*", a crash course by us, in how negotiations were done in this industry.
We were on a steep learning curve;
"*flying on the seat of our pants*".
In truth we had never planned to leave our existing brewery, we were merely using a competitor, to drive a better bargain, to assist us in negotiations. We were less than secret about meeting the new supplier, pretty certain our existing brewery had more than an inkling of what was going on.
However, changing circumstances can have unplanned repercussions, so a deal with the new brewery could go from a very unlikely proposition to a serious option, if our current brewery becomes intransigent during forthcoming talks.

We phoned our current brewery representatives and introduced ourselves, as the new senior negotiating team, on behalf of the Llanrwst RBL club, (neither of these companies have agreements with us, now 24 years later) to inform them we had found another supplier.
They asked for immediate talks and within days, the negotiating teams were assembled.
The Brewery representative said;
"They could not believe we wanted to leave, as relations with the last club committee had always been good for both parties,"
They were informed;
"We were paying too much for their beer and could get a better deal elsewhere
The beer we sold, was practically the same price as the pubs and we are not competitive. The economics from our viewpoint are simple, their competitors are offering a cheaper price, even based on current sales. They were also offering better rewards for increased sales.
A competitive price for our beers attracts more customers and

encourages more members to join the club. A vital part of the new committees strategy is membership growth, this is key to us having a successful business"

The talks broke down after a few hours, with the brewery saying; *"The current agreement, was non-negotiable and still had a period to run, which they expected us honour".*

Our response to this was;

"Contractually they can hold us to the existing agreement, but if we remain uncompetitive, the club will close and there will be no account to lose "

We also reminded them that;

"Once our agreement comes to an end, if we are still open for business, there is zero chance the club would stay with a brewery, so unsympathetic to our current plight."

The Royal British Legion Club circa 2000.

At the turn of the century, the club looked "tired" and that is putting it kindly. It was sold to the RBL London for £5 in 1969, by the then club committee. The RBL owners have not spent a penny on its upkeep since.

Chapter 14

Following the breakdown in talks with the brewery, David, Jerry and I discussed our options. Coming to the conclusion they doubted our claim, we had extracted such a good deal from a rival brewery and thought the deadline was a negotiating ploy, really no more than a *"bluff"* on our part.

Weeks passed, without contact, I was being encouraged to ring our existing brewery and seek fresh talks, as the deadline came closer. Having done many last minute deals, as a trade union official, in a previous life, it may have been easier for me, but the pressure was still intense.

Our new potential supplier was drawing up an agreement, awaiting a list of signatories from us, keen to get their contract finalised in the next few days.

During discussions at the bar, there was a lot of unease, we had only been in charge for a few weeks and questions were already being asked about our competence as senior officers.

"Why cause such havoc with the bank and brewery right from the offset, should we be less contentious, were we guilty of overplaying our hand."

Jerry explained

"In normal times, caution would be appropriate, but we don't have time on our side"

With the battle lines drawn, there was a lot riding on who blinked first.

The day before we were due to sign an agreement with our new supplier, Stan Roberts, our long serving senior member of staff contacted me to say;

"There was an urgent phone call from our brewery".

Returning the call, we learnt they wanted a further meeting.

We quickly assembled our team and agreed to meet that evening in the office above the club.

The meeting started as a tetchy affair, with comments from them about *"bad faith"*, *"unhonoured contracts,"* and *" the restoration of better relations"* dominating their early presentation, which was expected, given their reluctance to renegotiate with us.
We explained;

"It was our responsibility, to find the best deal on behalf of our members, and we made no apology for the tactics we used."
After this early sparring, we did get down to some meaningful negotiations in an improved atmosphere, without any further rancour.

We eventually came up with a similar agreement, to that agreed with their competitor, with barrel prices reduced based on current sales. Expected barrel price rises in the next few months were put on hold and rebates for hitting improved targets agreed.
This meant we would pay less now, for existing stock in the short term, and increased sales would see both parties sharing the benefits of growth in the long term.

It was a vastly improved offer and one we could recommend to the club committee.

When the brewery team had left, we retired to the bar, where Big Rich was waiting for news regarding the negotiations from his brother David.

Someone, looking slightly worse for wear was moidering Rich, which was going to end badly. He has a low tolerance level for such people, so putting his not inconsiderable frame between him and his brother, jostled him away, giving him some salient advice in the process.

A heavily edited version of his comments reads;

"Get your corpulent follicled arse out of the bar into the lounge and talk shit to the illegitimate coffin dodgers in there"
There tended to be a more senior clientele in the lounge and it's

certainly less confrontational than the bar, which we normally frequent.
Having removed the interloper, it was rumoured David said some complimentary things to Rich about my input into today's negotiations. Later that evening David resorted to type denigrating;
"my pathetic negotiating skills on display earlier today"
Which provided much merriment at my expense.
A special committee meeting the next day ratified the agreement, with the club staying with the existing brewery.
David then tells me;
"You're lucky to be in one piece "Pickwick", the people you have upset, without us (Rich and him) watching your back, you would be toast"
I pointed out;
"Without Jerry and the brothers Grimm roping me into their crazy cunning plans, I would not need minders, in the first place"

Now came the unenviable task of informing the representative from the competing brewery, we would not be signing the agreement, scheduled for later today, as we were staying with our existing supplier.
It is not the worst business phone call I've ever made, but it's way up there on the list.. To say he was not happy is a massive understatement, he was livid, understandably so, having come so close to signing a deal, with a new customer worth just short of £100,000 a year.
He angrily referred to my;
"illegitimacy" and *"untrustworthiness"*, while wishing me;
"a long and painful demise "
These were the gist of his remarks, the actual diatribe being unprintable.
When he had cooled down, he accepted that part of his job was

to ward off predatory approaches from other breweries, if they attempted to poach his customers.

Conversely he would have no problem undermining a competitor's long standing agreement, if it meant getting a new business opportunity for his employer.

We eventually found common ground agreeing, it was a cut throat business where the stakes are high and despite everything, it was nothing personal.

Trying to end the phone call in a conciliatory manner, I told him; *"Nothing is forever, so who knows what the future holds, we may well do business together in the coming years, so it was important the lines of communication remain open"*

Over the years, our paths have crossed a few times, once at a Brewery Industry Award Ceremony (which will feature later).

His career in the main has continued to have an upward trajectory, despite this unfortunate setback.

He jokingly now refers to the "*Llanrwst episode*" as the *"life skills element"* of his *"management training course."*

Not unexpectedly though, his Christmas card list, still has an obvious omission residing at Pickwick's Antiques and Tearoom.

Having my head shaved for the Testicular Cancer Charity

Edgar Parry make sure I don't chicken out, as my son Nathan wields the clippers

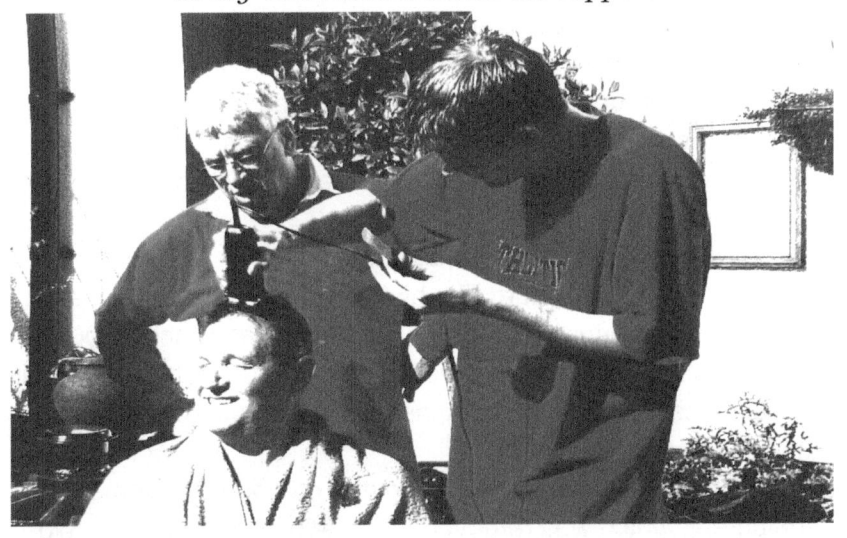

Someone suggested I looked like an East End villain

Chapter 15

Being a non profit organisation, registered as a friendly society at Companies House, means the club has *"charitable status"*. This provided some opportunities to reduce some bills, particularly with utility companies. We switched a number of business providers, (there was no comparethemarket.com.) which was a time consuming exercise.

Business rates were too high, so an appeal was lodged to reduce the rateable value. The higher the rateable value the more business rates you pay. It's a complicated process, but if you're successful (which we were) it also reduces the Sky TV bill, as business accounts are also geared to the rateable value of the property.

Interestingly we were paying a hygiene company for some equipment, which was removed years ago. We negotiated two years of credits with them, while not a lot of money, it was one less bill to pay.

There were cigarette machines in the club, ripping off customers selling a packet of "16" cigarettes, over and above the normal price of a packet of "20". The club received nothing from this, yet were expected to keep the cigarette dispensers topped up and maintain the machines.

David said;   *"If they don't pay us for the machines, they will be in a skip tomorrow"*.

The service provider had some harsh words to say about the new committee, as they collected the machines the next day. David, a non-smoker, was happier still in the knowledge:

"they preferred the previous management to us", which he rightly took as a compliment.

Free banking, lower rent and reduced brewery costs, would help the cash flow, but bills would increase in the run up to Christmas as we purchased more stock.

The entertainment for the Millennium celebrations had already been booked by our predecessors and was mind bogglingly expensive. Contractually it was too late to cancel, with the event only a few months away.
We decided to charge admission to cover the cost, which was very unpopular but unavoidable, in the situation we inherited.
The club, despite being filled to capacity, still made a loss on the last evening of the century, when set against staffing, entertainment and the cost of stock.
No one said that this mission, yes that's what it has become, would be easy, rejection by the bank, election malpractice and now problems with the millennium celebrations, did not bode well for the future.

It seemed that; *"Saint Jude, the patron saint of lost causes,"* had taken up permanent residence in Llanrwst club, but then another unforeseen problem arose. Bank paying-in books had arrived from our new bank, but not cheque books. The new committee's authority to close bank accounts and transfer direct debits was disputed by our former bank, who many believed were being deliberately obstructive.
We were able to pay the staff in cash, but some of our suppliers had to wait six weeks for cheques and direct debits before these difficulties were resolved.
No one could say this fledgling committee had so far led a charmed life, but this banking administration blunder unexpectedly provided a window of opportunity.
Money was coming in, but less is going out in the short term, as our suppliers and utilities waited for their bills to be paid.
Membership was growing, sales were increasing and the cash flow situation was looking healthier.

Chapter 16

Another day, another meeting at Pickwick's for the finance committee. Gill and I are thinking of charging Jerry and David for bed and breakfast, as they're here, more than our paying guests at the moment.
Jerry said;
"*He was spending more time on club business, than in his proper job*"
David claimed;
"*He has hardly seen his family for a month*"
Before getting down to business I reminded them;
"You pair roped me into this, against my better judgement and due to them, Pickwick's was fast becoming my part- time job".
The purpose of today's meeting was to assess how many members the club had and what figure was required, to make the club a viable business proposition again.
Unlike today (2024) where we have only 2 categories of membership, annual and temporary (1 month), there were many more under the the Royal British Legion. There were full members (ex- service), associate members (non- ex service) and in Llanrwst there were 150 retired ex service who had their subscriptions paid for by the RBL branch (despite this being against the rules). There were also Women Section members divided into full, associate and retired.
Once you have joined one of the various categories above, you were eligible to join the club paying £2 subs in 1999.
We estimated there were between 500 and 525 members currently on the club's books.
These membership figures are actually an overestimation, because many ex-service pensioners only attended the club

once a year, when picking up their £20 Christmas payment from the branch.

We concluded the club needed a minimum of 750 members, with a quarter of these being *"active"*, using the club as their main local. Membership generally was in decline, but more worrying was, many *"active"* members were also turning their back on the club.

Falling attendances were visually apparent, especially during midweek and this was also confirmed by lower bar receipts.

The club's demise was a combination of incompetent management and high overheads. In the long term we can reduce the rent and take the gaming machine back, but we have to be proactive to increase membership and sales.

The differential of 2p between the club and pub beer prices in Llanrwst is far too low, and is a handicap to membership growth. Sadly the previous committee knew the club was uncompetitive, but by announcing price increases just before being defeated in recent elections, were about to make the situation worse.

In 1999 the club was charging £1.67 for a lager and the previous committee were due to increase this to £1.77, in line with the other pubs in town who were also raising prices by 10p.

The new committee had no intention of honouring this commitment to increase prices. Our recent brewery settlement gave us the opportunity to be bold and radical in our approach and make a *"statement"* about the direction the club was going, both to our members and competitors.

That "statement" was to reduce, rather than increase the beers by 10p sending out a message that;

"The Club meant business"

Our beer will then be £1.57 a pint with a differential of 22p over our nearest competitor. Providing we increase wet sales, with this initiative, we believe the club's future could improve significantly.

Chapter 17

The brewery thought it was foolhardy of us to reduce prices so drastically, whether fearing for the club's future or fearing the loss of another customer, they clearly had no support for our radical business plan.

Our stocktaker conferred with the brewery's assessment advising us to put up prices. Over the years, every stocktake report indicates our percentage profits are inadequate and beer prices have to rise, even to the present day.

Being kind, we welcome their suggestions, but will keep our own counsel on these matters, given our recent unfortunate experiences with "*other experts*" from the legal and banking professions.

Jerry recalled how in the distant past;

"It was traditional for townsfolk to go round the pubs and end up finally at the club, where they bought several rounds, because the club sold cheaper beer. Maybe this will revive that tradition?"

David said; *"If this price cut drives up sales by 25% we can start building up our depleted bank account, it's risky but it might work, doing nothing is not an option"*

All those in favour say "*aye*", so the finance committee of Jerry, David and I gave it; *the "three ayes".*

We reconvened yet another club committee meeting, to howls of protest, promising this would be our last *"special"* meeting and possibly the most important meeting in our short reign to date. We outlined the problems with cash flow, explaining how these early setbacks would be overcome.

We were optimistic that the new millennium would see the club go from strength to strength. There was some scepticism about a plan to cut prices, but the general opinion was, this would produce a surge in recruitment, with the timing perfect with

membership renewals, due soon on October 1st 2000.
As treasurer my responsibility was to highlight the necessity to back the business plan, while making the committee aware of the reservations from the brewery, stocktaker and others.
The committee voted unanimously to approve the finance committee plans for the future and the reduction in prices would commence the next day. It was further agreed that we put large posters in the foyer and in each bar, highlighting the new prices members would pay. The meeting closed with Edgar Parry, the chairman urging committee members to;
"Spread the word, the club is on the way up, prices are coming down, so let's create some positive energy about the future of the club"

The same week a pub landlord complained that;
"The club would put him out of business with the beer reductions, as they were already struggling"
We explained that pubs are profit making businesses, while the club is there to serve its members, Breaking even is a poor business outcome for a pub whether it is owned by the landlord or if tenanted, but it's a reasonable aspiration for most clubs. Once the Llanrwst club is organised properly, and we still have a long way to go, it will always be cheaper than the pubs, not to put them out of business but to provide the members with affordable prices.
On a personal level, we did sympathise with the landlord's struggle and agree the town needs a mix of pubs and hotels along with the club. The fact remains though, our ambition is to make the club the best in North Wales
"If this comes to fruition, complaints will increase, because the inevitable consequences of our strategy for increasing membership is competitive pricing.

> *"If you're lost, you can look
> and you will find me
> time after time"*
> Cyndi Lauper
> " Time after time"

Chapter 18

We adjourned to the bar, where Ken Davies entertained us with some hilarious tales of his escapades while ferreting with Ted Thomas. He then said;
"It's great to have you guys David, Jerry and Mick leading the fight, on the members behalf, you're the Generals"
Pointing to the other committee members he continued;
"Were just the foot soldiers, making up the numbers"
Jerry, as usual, found the right words, with the right gravitas in his reply;
"You Ken, like Colin, Rich and others are not insignificant foot soldiers, quite the opposite, we feed off your support, you are vitally important to us. In fact you and the other committee members are the glue that keeps us together"
With harmony restored, Sheila Thompson accompanied by Shelley Winters joined us at the bar with Shelley challenging us on her pet issue;
"Now you guys are in charge, does this mean women are allowed to play on the snooker table"
This was met with a resounding;
"Yes, as of today, women can play snooker and that's official."

I regret this decision every time Fallon, Sheila's daughter, displays her superior skills when showing me up at snooker.

The evening was just ending, everyone was in good spirits, beer prices were coming down tomorrow and the news had spread like wildfire. It seemed like a cloud had been lifted, then David dropped another bombshell, or did;
"Saint Jude, the patron saint of lost causes strike again".
David had confiscated the *"branch hospitality book"* from behind the bar. He further demanded the balance owed to the club by the branch be paid up in full the next day..
He then winked at me and said;
"Will that will help the cash flow, Mr Treasurer?"

Jerry and I could not believe David's timing, given the multitude of outstanding issues we are dealing with already, but on reflection, at least the *"free drinks book"* can't mysteriously disappear now.
This confrontation was always going to happen one day, so just think of it as another item on the forever growing *"to-do"* list and deal with it. One thing is for sure, it's far from predictable or boring when Davd's around.
In response to David's actions, my in-tray "bulged", there were letters from the branch, correspondence from the district office and threats of legal action regarding the return of the *"branch hospitality book"*, which continued for months.
The Llanrwst RBL branch secretary wrote;
"Finally I am making a formal request for you to return the Branch Hospitality book as a matter of urgency. I would remind you that this is the property of the branch committee"
David on behalf of the committee gave an oral reply which stretched to two words containing a total of seven letters.

The new club committee will never allow free drinks for the branch officers or anyone else in the future, so the book is now obsolete. It's also evidence of wrongdoing and needs safekeeping for the future.

During the last few months, other committee records and files have mysteriously disappeared, the *"branch hospitality book"* will not suffer the same fate.

We had other important matters on our minds. Following negotiations with the branch the gaming machine was finally coming back to the club. It should never have been allowed to leave the club in the first place, and it's the new committee's absolute priority that the bandit is returned.

An agreement dated 1st october 1999 stated;

"The Royal British Legion branch hereby agree to transfer the gaming machine to the RBL Club Llanrwst subject to the following provisos; The club pay an annual rent of £8,400 and shall be responsible for all hire, licence and VAT."

On the 21st July 2000,10 months later, this agreement was still not honoured so Ken Jenkins, secretary wrote to the Branch;

"Every month that goes by, more money is transferred from the club to the branch, money you are not allowed to spend.

Given the lack of response from the branch, it has been decided, all information on the gaming machine, the issuing of free bottles, and both club and branch hospitality books, will be sent to the charity commission.

We will recommend they have an investigation, unless the branch is forthcoming on all outstanding matters relating to the club"

It is not all bad news, there are considerably more people using the club now since the introduction of lower prices. Bar receipts are up and membership figures have exceeded our target.. We

have now cleared the bank overdraft, while looking forward to receiving the keys to the branch bandit in the coming weeks.
The new Club Benevolent Fund set up for sport, charities and local good causes raises most of its income from raffles and football cards, sold during the club bingo. We need to grow this fund, having taken over much of the branch's responsibility in this area.
We as committee officers, were becoming more proficient as we grew into our respective roles, this was despite the RBL's failure to offer any training on how to manage a licenced property.
With the exception of a few, who were unlikely to be persuaded, the reservations most staff had about their new employers were disappearing as the club showed signs of improvement, and their job security fears dissipated.

The women's section were asked to contribute to the club's *"benevolent fund"* from their bingo, which they hold in the club once a week.
The club would continue to provide the room, heating and lighting for free and open the bar in the concert room for them to run their bingo session. The bar staff wages alone far exceed the bar takings from the women's section bingo night, so the club is already subsidising the women's section bingo.
This request for a contribution, bringing the branch bingo into line with the club's bingo, would make it fair for everyone.
The last thing we expected was;
"St Jude the Patron Saint of lost causes" would manifest itself again in the form of the Women's Section officers.

Chapter 19

The word came back, that the "women's section officers" were not happy with suggestions from the club, regarding the benevolent fund.

Given this opposition, the club requested a meeting with the women's section, and offered dates.

They suggested 10.00 pm, the club in 2000 was only open till 10.30 pm, so it was blatantly obvious they were not interested in any meaningful discussions.

We offered further dates, at more reasonable times but to no avail, they ignored our requests and didn't reply.

The RBL club lease allows the women's section to have office space in the club, we therefore wished to discuss access, office equipment, security, noticeboards, frequency of meetings, AGM arrangements, key holder responsibilities and any other matters they might wish to discuss. We were hopeful a dialogue would start in the interest of both parties.

We again had no reply, which led to a stand off, culminating in the *"women's section"* walking out and holding their bingo, in a rival pub in Llanrwst.

This was a completely unexpected development and judged by many, to be an overreaction, which should have been avoided. We can only guess what motivated the *"women section officers"* to do this, other than an attempt to weaken the club, that was just getting back on its feet.

It's been suggested we engineered this dispute, but nothing could be further than the truth, we were preoccupied on so many different fronts already. We neither had the time nor the inclination for a further disagreement, with our main focus being the financial well-being of the club.

Many members thought that the women's section leadership was contemptuous of the new committee, so were seeking revenge on behalf of the previous club committee. If this is true, their misplaced loyalty to former RBL officials was foolhardy in the extreme.

A week later, not content with organising a rogue bingo evening, the dispute escalated into a complete boycott of the club, organised by the *"women's section"* leadership.

Testing our patience further, some women members were dispatched to the club, hoping to borrow the club's bingo equipment, cards and raffles to use at the rival public house, as they had done the week before.

Their cheek was not rewarded, as they were given short shrift, when Jerry intercepted them during their quest, telling them;

"To purchase their own equipment, tickets and raffles".

An official RBL group organising an exodus of members from the club is unprecedented, and an immediate response was required. If we lose a large section of female members, it will damage the club's business growth strategy, just when we were moving towards financial stability.

We decided the club should hold both the Monday and Wednesday bingo sessions ourselves, as the women's section had now given up their usual bingo slot by default.

This would give an unexpected boost to the club's benevolent fund, as more raffles and football cards would be sold, providing many of those errant women members returned to the fold.

A notice was put up explaining how the dispute started and how efforts to resolve the situation had been ignored by the women's section officers, who seemed determined to damage the club and undermine the new club committee. We then inviting women to join the Llanrwst branch for the first time in its history, so they can;

"Play bingo and enjoy all the other benefits the club had to offer."

Ann Pritchard, Sheila Thompson and other women resigned from

the women's section to join the Llanrwst RBL branch (*which is open to both sexes*) and encouraged others to follow suit.
The response was overwhelming and we broke all recruitment records over the next few days, running out of application forms on several occasions.
The women's section officers could only look on in horror as over 150 applications were received from new members and former women's section members, all finding a new home in the Llanrwst RBL branch. The new club bingo night was a great success, drawing record attendances and paying out bigger prizes.
Following this, there were letters and phone calls from Wrexham RBL officials regarding the mass resignations from the women's section.
Not surprisingly we were the villains again and that word "*dissident*" came to prominence again as a *"Miss Marple"* type figure regaled Jerry, David and I in the club on Armistice day, where she was enjoying the buffet, freely provided by the club. She was a leading *"women's section"* official for North Wales, now unfortunately, leading an ever decreasing female section, because of *"dissidents"* like us.
Armistice was not the appropriate time for this discussion, so we chose not to engage with her. We actually had some sympathy with her; "*because through no fault of her own*", she had lost 95% of her membership in Llanrwst due to the incompetence of her local officials.
Having been called a lot worse than *"dissident"* during the last few years, we are getting quite attached to our new *rebellious label*.
Attempts at mediation did arrive at an understanding, if not an agreement after the involvement of regional RBL officers.
We agreed that;
"Anyone who wished to transfer back to the women's section

could and we would provide forms to fill in and process them on their behalf"

Not a single person took up the offer, despite notices to this effect being posted on all notice boards. This badly organised protest, designed to undermine the club by the *"women's section"* officers, lasted two weeks, as did their *"rebel bingo"*, before petering out.
They chose the issue and timing of the dispute, which was not dissimilar to the previous club committee's *"ballot debacle"* which also ended in an embarrassing defeat.
Both these failed campaigns, lacked leadership and strategy;
"*They were both a masterclass in ineptitude"*

A van used for our family business, Pickwick's Antiques while parked in the Victoria Hotel car park, (with permission from Kay King) was vandalised, with the window wipers and wing mirrors also being snapped off.
A friend from the club, mechanic Gwyn (Burgess) Jones always did our MOT's and repairs, although very rarely when promised. His excuses were legendary." *Burgess time"* was flexible as was *"tomorrow"* which had a tolerance of up to a week or more. Burgess truly ran a *"24 hour let down service "* but on hearing of the damage, which he firmly believed was related to disputes in the club, had the parts ordered and fitted within days. He also refused any payments, as he was so disgusted by the whole incident.
Big Rich, who never missed a chance to get in a telling barb, said;
"Get over yourself, Mick Pickwick, it's your own fault courting unpopularity, the police already have 500 suspects for the attack on your van, with figures expected to rise in the coming weeks".

Anonymous Cartoon circa 2000 posted on the
Llanrwst Kwik Save (now Coop)
supermarket notice board

Giving ex-service OAP's money at Christmas
(a practice, much abused) came to an end
during my 4 year term as treasurer.
It was obviously not to everyone's liking.
It seems I have also acquired two builder's
bums in this less than flattering cartoon.

Chapter 20

During 2001 and 2002, the club's finances improved beyond all expectations with membership growing to over 800. The gamble the club made, in reducing prices, increased sales by over 24%. The overdraft is now paid off and there is £30,000 in the bank, much of this coming from the second bandit, which has finally returned to the club.
The branch has withdrawn its compensation claim for handing the gaming machine back, which is just as well, since David demanded the keys and the club refused to pay, unsurprisingly given the hundreds of thousands of pounds the branch has squandered over many decades.
It's taken over 30 years, but at last, the club now has two bandits and a recently acquired a lotto machine, which will further improve the clubs cash flow.
A new system was put in place allowing any member to come in on a saturday morning to observe the emptying and counting of money from the various machines.
The branch (landlord) bowed to our demands to reduce the rent from £8,400 to £3,600 and relationships with the branch have now become harmonious. (or so we thought)

It has been an embarrassment for years that there are no disabled toilets in the Llanrwst club. The branch failed to get grants from the National Lottery or from the RBL to build one. Visiting disabled ex-service veterans were shocked by the lack of facilities in Llanrwst club,caused by our predecessors, who had failed to prioritise this issue.
The branch had the money to fund this itself and should have waved protocol, gone ahead, knowing the RBL was unlikely to censure them for spending funds on this vital facility.

With the Irish Wheelchair Association visiting Llanrwst for the first time, later this year, the club were determined not to disappoint them, so decided to fund and erect the toilet themselves.
The timescale only left weeks, in which to build the toilet, after planning permission was approved.
It was touch and go, like a scene from *"DIY, SOS," (without Nick Knowles)* as Bobby Dean, Colin Owen, Jerry, Rich and David crawled all over each other in the confined space in a frantic attempt to get the facility built on time.
Everyone gave their time for free, finishing days before our Irish friend's arrival. These visits continued for the next 20 years, up until Covid struck. It was a joy to behold, hearing their musicians play while watching our Irish guests dancing in their wheelchairs.

The club licensing prior to 2003, was overseen by magistrates, the legislation had clubs closing at 10.30 in the evening, with no *"open all day"* provisions, as there are now. Any variation required a visit to the magistrate court, for an *"extension of hours"* or permission for a *"private function"*.
We inherited a system, where all this was done by a solicitor, who was paid an annual retainer for looking after the licence and for each variation to normal hours. During the course of time, we learnt we could attend the court in person ourselves, and do this much cheaper.
Common practice saw most solicitors bypass this process, contacting the magistrates clerk by Fax, which they did on a regular basis. After a while we too, were faxing our requests for *"licence variations"* without the need for legal representation.
This left the solicitor with one function;
"To ensure the club had a licence and it was up to date".
We never thought that;
"St Jude the patron saint of lost causes"
Would make another appearance in the form of a solicitor.

The club received a letter from The Court of Justices, Llandudno, during early July 2002 informing us;
"That the club licence had expired".
We examined the files we inherited, but could find nothing relating to the licence.
Random mishaps and unforeseen obstacles were appearing too regularly for them to be coincidental. Were there people with alternative motives, determined to stop the progress we were making?
Were there marginalised groups who preferred the club closed, rather than be managed by the current committee, you do have to wonder?
The previous officers of the club, must have known the licence was expiring, but they;
"chose to stay silent".
Without a licence the club could not trade.
Why did our solicitors, who were paid a retainer, fail to inform us the licence, which then lasted 5 years, needed to be renewed?
Licensing today (2024) lasts in perpetuity, so there is no renewal process.

The Finance Committee, David *"grump"* Jerry "bach" and I asked for an urgent meeting with our solicitor. It was arranged for the next day.
We asked him;
"How can a situation arise, where Llanrwst Club is left without a licence to trade, when we pay you a retainer, to look after licencing matters on our behalf"
He said; *"They have a policy of not telling clients, when the licence needs renewing"*
We asked him to repeat this, because his reply seemed incredulous.
*"We have a policy of not telling you, but there is a logical reason

for this which he was happy to explain"
Jerry interjected, demanding clarification.
"So let's be clear, you knew the licence was due and you chose not to inform the secretary, is that right?
"Yes, but" David stopped him again, he was furious.

"Before you give us the reasons for your incompetence, are you aware, the club will be forced to close down? It will take 28 days to get a new licence. We can renew, but there will be a gap between the end of the current licence and the court registration certificate hearing. We have talked to several Llanrwst pub landlords, because it is possible to include the club on their licence on a temporary basis. To date every publican has refused to assist us, some even taking great pleasure in our discomfort "
The solicitor then explained;
"Some years ago a solicitor in Llandudno, had failed to inform a private club their licence was due. This resulted in the club shutting down, for a lengthy period of time.. The social club successfully brought a court action against the solicitor for loss of earnings due to professional negligence."
A caucus representing solicitors, met to discuss how they could avoid this happening again in the future.
Their caucus's solution was;
"Clients would be told that it was no longer the solicitors responsibility to inform them, when their licence was due. That's how we came to have a policy of not telling clubs or pubs when their licence was due"
Seeking a further explanation, we asked;
"Will you confirm that the only service you now provide to the club is "the renewal of the licence"; He replied; *"Yes"*
"So in short, we are paying you, not to tell us when our licence is due, is that right?" I remarked
He had no answer for this.
We left him in no doubt that we held him responsible, saying;

"If you did your job properly, a caucus of local solicitors would not need a policy to cover up their incompetence"
As we left, we stated;
"We now have a policy of not paying incompetent so-called professionals, and will close the account today, you won't be missed, as your doing sweet FA anyway.
Llanrwst RBL club will also consider writing to the Law Society to complain about the poor service you provide".
Going out the door, David said rather loudly;
"What do you call a shipping tragedy resulting in 600 lawyers being lost at sea?"
Jerry and I replied in perfect harmony *"a good start".*
On returning to the office, Cath and Sheila were busy, writing cheques, posting them off to suppliers, cheques were more common than Direct Debits at that time. As luck would have it, the solicitor's name was spotted by Jerry on an envelope, so he said;
*" Don't send those b******* a cheque, they will never get another penny from the club."*
Other than for conveyancing, to my knowledge, no solicitor's have been used by the club since.
The mention of a *"caucus"* reminded me of an old adage from my trade union past;
"What is the difference between a caucus and a cactus?"
The answer, never more relevant than in this case;
"With a cactus, the pricks are on the outside"
The club will be ever grateful to Jim and Veronica Gordon, publicans of the New Inn, Llanrwst, who allowed the club to trade from their drinks licence for four weeks, whilst the paperwork, for our Registration Renewal Certificate, was presented to the magistrate court. Without their help the £30,000 in the business account would have been wiped off, if we went a month without trading.

> *"But I don't feel afraid,*
> *as long as I gaze at Waterloo sunset*
> *I am in paradise"*
> *Kinks*
> *" Waterloo Sunset"*

Chapter 21

As Club treasurer, I was asked on behalf of the club committee to examine every possible avenue open to us, to regain the ownership of the club, from the branch.

The club bought the building, with a loan in March 1968 for £5000 and donated it to the branch in 1973.

The club then became the tenant paying the British Legion branch (the new landlord) a peppercorn rent of £5 per annum. Remarkably the club were still paying off the brewery loan when this agreement was signed.

The RBL constitution only allows this business transaction to take place, if a meeting of all members are firstly consulted and then agree *"en masse"* to this undertaking.

There is no record of such a meeting taking place.

We asked the parents/ grandparents of current members if they had any knowledge of this meeting. Not a single person from that era remembers this historic event and no records exist in the club or branch to confirm this transaction.

It is our strong belief, the officers at the time signed their club away, without the members consent.

Unsurprisingly, the handwritten minute book for 1970 to 1975 was not among the archive material we inherited in 1999. The RBL head office is unable to confirm whether the full membership were consulted as stated in the rules.

Their claim that officers signed the club away 50 years ago is irrefutable because the Royal British Legion head office furnished us with copies of the signed document, on request. The wording states that the British Legion head office will hold the deeds in trust on behalf of the Llanrwst branch.

Who gave the authority to the Club officials to effectively give the club away remains a mystery?

What logical reason did the club have for handing over the deeds to the branch and why was it kept secret from the members remains unclear?

It has been suggested that there were tax advantages to the club in donating the building. Our research finds no evidence to substantiate this as both entities, the branch and club have charitable status and the club has *"friendly society"* status at Companies House where it is registered as a *"not for profit"* organisation.

Despite the wording, head office, not the branch are the owners of the club and have been since 1973. Nothing we have heard from them to date, indicates they are willing to alter the status quo.

While the lease arrangements have become manageable at a low of £3,650 a year following negotiations with the new committee, they were at times a huge burden, once the peppercorn rent of £5 a year was consigned to history.

That £5 a year rent grew to a high of £25,000 a year paid to the branch (or the income from the gaming machine) In 30 years, that's over half a million pounds in rent the club has paid the branch.

If the peppercorn rent agreement had been honoured, the club would have paid £150, not half a million pounds, during that period.

It begs the question:

" *What happened to all that money and what could the club have*

achieved, if freed, from the burden of debt for all those years?"
The club committee has examined every possible avenue to restore their rightful ownership of the Kings Head without success. We have now reluctantly conceded defeat, closing this dark chapter in the club's history.
Maybe one day in the future, the club will again own the building, it may be a forlorn hope, but it will forever be the club committee's ambition.
It will not be in my time, as my tenure as treasurer and committee member is coming to an end, with the club debt free, with money in the bank and a bright future beckoning for my successor.

The new harmonious relationship with the branch, was short lived and no one was surprised, when the club was disadvantaged once again by the branch's actions
The Club was hopeful that the £40,000 in the branch account, all of which came from their former ownership of a gaming machine, could be transferred back to the club.
This also, unfortunately, had a disappointing outcome.
The branch officers transferred most of this money to the national COIF charity fund, once there, it was impossible to access. We are led to believe, the current branch committee have decided not to contest the next annual elections, donating the £40,000, being their departing shot and final insult to the club.

The Antique Snooker Table by makers E A Claire

*"Snooker in Wales had become a contact sport, limping home, bruised in some unmentionable places was a common occurrence.
It was more dangerous than playing rugby, avoiding injury became the height of my ambition".*
Mick Bucknall

Chapter 22

On a more promising note, the club's new benevolent fund has been boosted of late when Jerry(bach) hosted a *"Horse Racing Night"* raising £1000. I never quite matched that, organising *"An Auction"* with Gill, donating surplus stock from our antique shop. Members also contributed kitchen equipment, bicycles, gardening equipment, toys, books and many other items.
Doing my stint as auctioneer, you could not help noticing that Ianto Thomas was buying most of the lots.
After the auction finished, he could not believe the amount of *"lots"* he had successfully bid for. To his credit he took a few things home, while donating the rest to various local charities.
It is important we grow the Benevolent fund, as the club now pays out the Christmas money to all ex service members. It also provides gifts to people in hospital and organises the annual mystery tour.
The only mystery about our predecessor's tour was;
"Why did they always go to Rhyl?"
There was no shortage of committee members, volunteering to hand out Xmas gifts of £20 from the club benevolent fund.
Big Rich, David, Jerry, Edgar, Ken Davis and Sheila all played "Santa" dishing out £3,000 in cash to pensioners, on the Saturday before Christmas.
Unsurprisingly,"*muggins here*" in need of some reputational enhancement, missed this rare opportunity to be popular for a day, spending three hours in the office instead, arguing with British Gas, having waited an eternity to get through.
David, in his usual festive mood said;
"Pickwick is always skiving off, when there's real work to be done, been asleep in the office again have you, Lazy b*******."
Some happy Xmas gift recipients have rewarded my committee friends with drinks for their sterling efforts today dishing out free

cash. I wished them all a Merry Christmas unenthusiastically, before returning the 100 yards to the Bucknall clan at Pickwick's Antiques and Tearoom to do my proper job.

During the payment of Xmas cash, it was noted letters were coming in from all over the UK, requesting money for OAP members. We also had people turning up with multiple membership cards claiming money for relatives living hundreds of miles away. Investigating further, we found many claimant's, only link with the club, came from joining, while on holiday in Llanrwst, but as ex- service pensioners, they fitted the narrow criteria for payments.

A lady from Llanrwst joined 7 ex service members to the branch (all qualifying for free membership while living in Yorkshire). She presented their membership cards claiming £140 which was paid. It was impossible to confirm whether they were ex-service, or if they even existed.

Particularly galling, was the sight of members, picking up their Xmas money, then leaving to spend it in another pub.

Jim and Veronica at the New Inn, said the Xmas payout day was always a great day for business. We didn't begrudge them, given they saved the club considerable money, when the club licence ran out, but other pubs were doing very well, thanks to our generosity.

Make no mistake, changes were afoot.

At the next finance committee, David, Jerry and I decided it was crazy handing out money, which was being spent in other drinking establishments. Next year we would introduce vouchers to use in the club instead of cash. We also introduced cinema tickets for member's children as we felt, everything was geared to older members.

Not everyone was keen on the vouchers scheme, those retired ex- service members, not living locally were unable to take up the offer. The £3000 spent previously, was reduced by half with this simple change. Even Llanrwst residents failed to claim their vouchers ,because many had never entered the club, other than to pick up the Christmas payout in the past.

As ex service membership declined over the years, Christmas payments were eventually phased out altogether. The club committee concentrated their energy on giving all members equal benefits and keeping the prices competitive.

The branch, despite advice to the contrary, from RBL district office had continued to pay ex service, retired members subscriptions on their behalf. After surrendering the bandit back to the club, the branch had no immediate source of income, so were forced to abandon the practice as their money was quickly running out.

This is no different to thousands of other RBL branches across the UK, surviving on hundreds, rather than many thousands of pounds. The Llanrwst branch will have to adapt to its new situation and budget accordingly.

Every club member now, regardless of whether they are ex-service, civilian, male or female will pay the same, and get the same benefits.

It was £10 to join the branch and £2 to join the club in 2000. This led to 50 ex-service members not renewing their (previously free) membership.

Despite losing these members, successful recruitment more than compensated for this, taking the total membership to 830. The demographics were also changing, as the average age of the membership fell and the percentage of women members increased.

Chapter 23

Things were going well, problems were becoming less frequent and relationships between the management and staff had been very good under secretary Ken Jenkins supervision.
"*St Jude the patron saint of lost causes was conspicuous by his absence*"
Then came another "bombshell".
Out of the blue, Ken Jenkins, announced;
"*His business interests were becoming more time consuming and he therefore felt he had no choice, but to step down as club secretary*".
Ken informed us;
"*He would continue as the poppy organiser for the RBL, buts thats all.*"
Nothing we said weakened his resolve to dedicate more time to his business, so we had to accept and respect his decision.
The Committee thanked him for the sterling work he had done for the club over the years.
Unbeknown to me David and Jerry, were aware of Ken's resignation, in advance of the meeting and had already discussed how the club could move forward from this, while acknowledging that Ken would be badly missed.

Jerry apparently said to David;
"*The finances are looking great, we have new systems in place, maybe it's time for Mick Pickwick to move on from treasurer and become secretary, a job he did as a trade union official, so being ideally suited to the role, with your Sheila taking on the treasurer's roll from Mick*"
David allegedly said
"*Mick only agreed to help sort the clubs finances out, then, he wants to concentrate on his greasy spoon cafe and junk shop, he

will never agree to be Secretary."
David was right. If we think of the club, as a company, with a turnover of £200,000, with the club secretary as the CEO, in charge of the board, (club committee) it helps to understand the club secretary's role and structure.
The buck stops with the secretary, it's a huge responsibility, overseeing policy and managing the business, while having responsibility for 11 employees. It was not something I had considered or wanted under any circumstances.
Jerry told David he had;
"A cunning plan to overcome my reservations"

At the next committee, Jerry said to me;
"We need a replacement for Ken Jenkins as secretary, you would be the ideal replacement having managed a trade union office and run your own business"
I gave a two word reply in the negative.
Jerry undeterred continued
"Just do the role of secretary for a year, help Sheila Thompson. settle in as treasurer, then review the situation in a years time, there will be no pressure to continue as secretary after the initial 12 months period"
"No, No, No, definitely not" was my instant reply.
There was a lot of flattery directed from some unusual quarters, even Big Rich was being positively pleasant to me, which was a first and worrying experience.
"No, No, No" became" maybe", As I fell for Jerry's line, with a ringing endorsement from everyone, distorting my better judgement.
"One year only, then you better find someone else " I said.
This was due to be my last meeting, with my treasurership terminating along with my resignation from the committee, this

very day.
So I gave my final financial presentation as planned.

Treasurer's report for 2002

Nearly 4 years on from taking on the treasurer's role, we have a new bar installed, have paid off the overdraft, created a new benevolent fund, now containing £5000 and taken the club to a healthy financial position.

The club accounts 1999 bank balance £0.000
2000 £24,000
2001 £64,918
2002 £81,671

This was achieved with only two 10p price rises during the last 4 years. Good as these figures look, a recent club survey identified £150.000 of outstanding building works, including the flat above the club which needs a total refurbishment.

There is no complacency however, if the large flat roof above the entertainment room needs replacing, it could cost £50,000.

Future investment in the infrastructure, new security doors, a new cellar refrigeration unit, heating system, and a £40,000 estimate, for an upgrade for the front of the building, are just some of the challenges the club faces.

To avoid the mistakes made by our predecessors, there is no plan to borrow from the bank or brewery for these costly projects. We must avoid a *"buy now, pay later culture"* and live sufficiently within our means.

Thank you for all the support I received as the club treasurer. It's been a sharp learning curve for everyone on the committee but I have every confidence Sheila will continue this good work in the future as the new club treasurer.

The original closing paragraph of my final financial report was supposed to be a *"goodbye"*, but *"events"* again intervened so these words below, will be saved till next year when my 12 months tenure as the temporary secretary comes to an end;

"It *has been a wonderful experience working with the finance committee Jerry and David and under the chairmanship of Edgar Parry and the rest of the management committee.*
We started as colleagues, but quickly became friends as we steered the club through the most testing and turbulent times.
Good luck to everyone, keep up the good work.
I am confident the club is in good hands to continue this success into the future."

Pickwicks Hotel and Tearoom
Pickwicks was where it all started with a visit to the courtyard by David (grump) Hughes and Jerry (bach) Thomas (1996) with a "cunning plan" to save the club from closure.

> " Its nine o'clock on a Saturday,
> the regular crowd shuffles in.
> there's a old man sitting next to me
> makin love to his tonic and gin."
> Billy Joel
> "Piano man"

Chapter 24

Harold Macmillan, UK Prime Minister was once asked;
"What was the greatest challenge"
He replied *"events dear boy, events"*
Unexpected *"events"* were becoming our staple diet.
"St Jude the patron saint of" lost causes"
was back, rampant as ever with the branch threatening the club's very existence once again in 2003.
Having come through a financial scare which threatened the future of the club, tackled the disappointment of a lost election, only to find the club had no licence to trade, we are nothing if not resilient, but this latest setback however will test our resolve even more.
You cannot have a Royal British Legion club, without first having a Royal British Legion branch.
The branch currently have 100 ex-service members and over 700 associate members;
Those 100 ex-service members have to fill the vacancies for branch officers. Without an elected branch committee, the club must close under the RBL rules.
There were 12 branch committee vacancies to fill including officers. Only 3 people have put their names forward, leaving 9 vacancies to fill, yet despite lots of arm twisting, no others could be persuaded to fill these vacant positions.

We have dealt with so many setbacks over the last 4 years;*"Hard hats should be mandatory at our club committee meetings",*
The branch's failure is just another example of the RBL's ineptitude, having no regard for the consequential damage it causes.
"How could a club, enjoying its most successful year, go out of business, through no fault of its own?
What options do we have, to avoid this pending catastrophe?"
We cannot close and re-open as a private club because the building is owned by the RBL, who would never countenance this option
The district office at Wrexham could act as a holding branch, with all Llanrwst members registering with them.
This can only be a temporary fix for 12 months, If after a year, no branch committee can be formed, the club would still have to close. The building would then be sold, with the proceeds of the sale going into the RBL's national funds.
We have no confidence that in 12 months time those branch positions will be filled, in fact, there will be even less ex-service members in a year's time, as it is the most rapidly declining section of our membership.
An urgent meeting between the club and district officials was convened to discuss the crisis, which threatened the jobs of our staff and the loss of a 50 year old community asset.
So how do you solve the following conundrum?
"Without a Royal British Legion branch committee there can be no Royal British Legion club"
Following hours of negotiations, we came up with a unique formula, approved by the RBL district office, later rubber stamped by RBL head office in Pall Mall, London.
"The Llanrwst club committee members would also serve as the Llanrwst branch committee, until a branch committee could be

elected. *This agreement, if acceptable, would be reviewed in 10 years time in 2013."*
The controversial part of this agreement was;
"The officers were effectively landlord and tenant and the same people would be in charge of the members welfare and club administration.
While this is highly controversial and more than questionable under the RBL rules, there were no further options open to us, to save the club.
Hence the new branch committee were as follows;
Mr K J Davies President, Mr E Parry, Chairman, Mr J Thomas, Vice Chairman, Mr M J Bucknall, Secretary, Ms S Thompson, Treasurer, Branch Committee Members, Mr A Roberts, Mr N Brabham, Mr J G Evans, Mr D Hughes, Mr R Parry, Mr J I Roberts and Mr C W Jones.
While the club committee would be the same people, each committee would meet separately and work independently producing their own minutes.

The closing balance on the branch accounts was £5,986, a long way from the £ 69,000, it had when the club had no money and almost went bankrupt.
My thoughts go back to that sunny day 7 years ago, when David (Grump) and Jerry (Bach) hijacked me in the courtyard with this ridiculous idea to change the direction of the club before it went bust.

From the outside it may look like we have spent years planning with Machiavellian precision, the removal of the old branch, the demise of the old club committee, along with the decimation of the woman's section membership.Nothing could be further from the truth. In the main, all we did was react to *"events"*, nothing illustrates this more than the *"bungled election"* or *"the women's*

section bingo walk out"
Our tactical abilities have been much overstated, there was no master plan and its beyond the realms of credibility that we could have foreseen how *"events"* would unfold.

The District office, hardly sympathetic to our cause, in the past, is now happy for the club committee to replace the old branch committee, made up of "dissidents" and their supporters.

Many would say it's been a good day, being part of the team that have ensured the survival of the club, and yes, there is a sense of pride and satisfaction, but a few days ago my treasurership was about to end, signing off, with:

"Mission accomplished with a clean break from any club or branch responsibilities"

Weeks later after emphatically saying *"No, No, No"* to being secretary of the club, I now find myself, secretary of the RBL branch and club overloaded with responsibilities, with twin secretarial duties and double the amount of problems piling up in my in-tray.

Jerry has a lot to answer for;

"with his cunning plans."

Experience tells me there is only ever one outcome, resulting from his *"hair-brained ideas'* that is;

"Short term temporary solutions I agree too, become never ending long term commitments"

I dread to think what my long suffering wife, Gill is going to say when I break the news that;

"My impending retirement from office has taken an unexpected turn today, which might require a little more of my time than previously forecast"

*Llanrwst Cricket club is a credit to the town with its activities for all ages ranging from adults to girls and boys.
Clwb Llanrwst Club is proud of its long association.*

Chapter 25

After years of letters and phone calls from the club committee, asking for an investigation into years of overpayment of rent, misuse of charitable funds and gaming machines irregularities by our predecessors, we were surprised to receive a reply at last.
It was a request from the Royal British Legion national investigation team to meet the club's senior officers, to conduct an investigation on behalf of the head office.
Three distinguished senior representatives came to Llanrwst club to meet the club's four senior officers. We had reams of evidence to present, and were well prepared, when their chairman opened the meeting.
It would not be the Llanrwst British Legion club, if things went smoothly and according to plan and this was going to be no exception.
The stern looks on their faces indicated this was going to be a confrontational and difficult meeting.
Unbelievable as it seems, they were not there to deal with our complaints, their specific, *"Terms of Reference"* were to;
"Conduct an investigation into complaints about "our activities at the Royal British Legion"
The *"our"* specifically, were David Hughes, Jerry Thomas, Edgar Parry and Michael Bucknall " *the Llanrwst dissidents"* who were the bad guys under investigation.
We were not told who the complainants were, or whether they were members, former club officials, branch officers, district or regional officials.
Our accusers, we established, were to remain anonymous.

We spent several hours answering their questions and providing them with financial accounts for the club, from before and after our involvement. We insisted on telling our story of a dominant branch, almost forcing the club out of existence.

We outlined the history of the *"peppercorn rent"*, subsequent rent increases, gaming machine irregularities and the misuse of funds over the years.

They seemed genuinely shocked at the account of the bogus election and the repeated lies, later retracted;

"We wanted to change the RBL club into a Labour club",

It was a civil, well conducted meeting, considering we nearly walked out, when the terms of reference, centred on our alleged wrongdoing. The meeting adjourned and we went downstairs to the club bar, while they carried on with their deliberations in private.

After an hour, or so, we were called back.

Their chairman then amazed us all with a statement;

"Can I first apologise on behalf of the Royal British Legion for coming to investigate you today. You have been treated badly, by the organisation, who at every level, put obstacles in your way, when your intentions were honourable.

The financial accounts are immaculately presented and it's possible to see the progress the club has made year by year since the new committee's involvement.

They commented on the noticeboards, which have up to date information for members, which they rarely see on their visits to establishments around the country.

They further explained, they will be making a report to the head office, saying;

"There is no case to answer."

They continued:

"Acting as whistleblowers, bringing wrongdoing and

mismanagement to RBL's attention, is commendable, we should have listened and had proper processes in place to manage these issues"

After much shaking hands, followed by some kind words from our visitors, the meeting came to an end and our guests departed.

Gobsmacked best describes our response as a stunned silence permeated the meeting room as they made their exit.

We assume a report will be sent to the head office and our district office exonerating us from any misdemeanours, we supposedly committed. Not only were we unaware of the charges against us, we still have no idea who instigated the inquiry. Hopefully the person responsible for sending these senior officers to Llanrwst RBL on *"a wild goose-chase"* will face severe repercussions for their ineptitude..

David spoke for us all, when summing up today's meeting;

"They are the first people from the RBL, that have ever had a good word to say about us, they were sent to reinforce the view, that we were the problem, not the solution, but were open minded enough to make a judgement exonerating us"

So the investigation we requested is not going to happen now or in the future, but it is still a matter of concern that our genuine grievances have been swept under the carpet, yet bogus claims against us have attracted the highest level of scrutiny the RBL has at its disposal.

You can only assume, those instigating the investigation, hoped this would see Jerry, David, Edgar and I exposed as troublemakers, excluded from membership and disbarred from office.

The irony is ailing clubs and branches are closing on an unprecedented scale while Llanrwst has booked that trend, increasing membership and running a successful club business.

"The powers that be" should be promoting Llanrwst as an *"example of excellence".*
Having been heaped with unexpected praise today for a change, by our distinguished guests, it brought home to me the unrewarded work that goes on behind the scenes in the club. Much more deserving of recognition are the unsung heroes, we take for granted;
Bobby Dean who is in the club most mornings, checking electrics, bulbs, replacing old wiring, along with Jerry and Dave, who are maintaining or repairing hundreds of items from door handles to toilet bowls, before the club opens.
They are there Saturday morning, along with Sheila and Stan emptying the bandits, lotto machine, jukebox, snooker and pool tables. To many people the club opens at 12.00, but there are hours of preparation and cleaning to do before the doors open. It's unrelenting, for 365 days a year, the staff are working to give our members a good experience, in a clean and safe environment.

The unexpected praise we received from the RBL hierarchy today did not last long, we were quickly brought down to earth, coming under attack again.
For waiting in the wings was;
"St Jude, the patron saint of lost causes, now appearing in female form, dressed in the finest regal ermine robes

Chapter 26

The local paper ran a front page headline;
"Llanrwst Armistice was being anglicised at the expense of the Welsh language".
This came from Baroness Christine Humphreys.
The new RBL branch, now run by club committee officers, is responsible for all aspects of Armistice, so this complaint questions the competence of the new committee. It's also a very serious accusation, disrespecting the Welsh language and you have to wonder which individual(s) from the committee are being targeted and why?
The article was the first contribution made by the baroness about the club, so it's a shame she took that opportunity to attack hard working volunteers. Those being criticised, give up their time for free, unlike her who is handsomely rewarded from the public purse.
She is entitled to her opinion, but it is incumbent on her when making serious allegations to get her facts right.
Edgar Parry, chairman and Ken Davies, president, organise Armistice for the branch, both are Welsh speakers.
They assured the committee that not one word had been changed from the church service, or the proceedings at the cenotaph.
The Vicar also confirmed there had been no variation to the previous format used over many years.
As Secretary I contacted the newspaper;
"Accusing them of cheap journalism"
It would only have taken a single phone call to the church, or

myself, to establish the truth, before writing this article.
The paper agreed to publish a letter from the RBL branch secretary setting the record straight.
A less than prominent, letters page denial from me, did little to dispel the damaging headline from the week before.
We wrote to Christine Humphreys to complain.
She wrote back to us, but there was one glaring omission in her response, and that was the absence of *"an apology"*.
It is very simple;
"Sorry the story was untrue"
Those five words would have done.
The volume of vitriol and abuse I received as a direct result of her comments was no surprise, the anglicised RBL branch secretary, was always likely to bear the brunt of any criticism, resulting from her comments.
Who were they to believe, an Honourable Peer from the House of Lords or a bunch of *"commoners"* on the RBL committee.
The RBL Llanrwst committee took the view that If Christine's false accusation warranted a headline, her non apology deserved equal prominence.
There was however, no front page rebuttal, just a retraction on the letters page, the gist of it being, it was;
"a result of circumstances"
"<u>Language critic praises town's Royal British Legion stalwarts</u>".
Following my criticism of the lack of Welsh input, into the public act of Remembrance in Llanrwst. I have been in correspondence with their secretary and am now content that this was surely a result of <u>circumstances</u> and no slight was intended on the Welsh language.
The British Legion is fortunate that Llanrwst has now produced a new generation of people, who give so generously of their time, contributing to the organisation locally and nationally and continuing its work into the future" Christine Humpheys

Chapter 27

Six years ago,(1999) the Annual General Meetings (AGM) attracted huge numbers, especially when the club was on the brink of closure, so there is no complacency amongst the membership, when a crisis occurs, the bigger the calamity the larger the turnout.

Now there are barely a dozen people attending these annual gatherings, as apathy sets in. Disappointed as we are, by these low turnouts, they may signify a contentment amongst members, who see no need to participate in annual meetings, while things are going well.

For those that read the notice boards, which is not many, there is no lack of information, members have never been so well informed, so maybe the AGM's have become superfluous for them.

We will of course continue to have AGM's as they are a legal requirement.

A much used phrase in the club is;

"If you want to keep a secret put it on the noticeboard".

If you have spent almost all your adult life attending committees of one type or another, both in my past life as a trade union officer and now as a club and branch secretary, don't expect any thanks, or you will be very disappointed.

You will be constantly reminded of any errors or indiscretions you've made regardless how small. It's a thankless task, but someone has to do it.

Never satisfying everyone, is summed up by an old story, from my trade union days;

A shop steward reporting back from a meeting with management addresses the workforce;

"I have managed to double your pay today, backdated for 5 years. Overtime will now be paid at triple the previous rate. The

retirement age will be reduced to 35 years of age and pensions doubled. Holidays will now increase to 12 weeks, paid at double time. Finally the working week is reduced to one day, so we only work Tuesdays.
A chorus of dissent rose as the crowd shouted;
"What every fxxxxxx Tuesday"
"Failure has a long memory, success is fleeting ".

There is plenty of banter in the club and unsurprisingly a little mild nationalism creeps in at times. A Welsh friend unhappily, watching an English rugby referee, supposedly being biassed against the Welsh team playing France, turned to the nearest Englishman (Me) to vent his anger;
"You made me wear the Welsh Not ".
The *"Welsh Not"* was a practice that started around 1840 and carried on to the 1940's;
"Whereby school children were punished for speaking Welsh. If caught they would wear a plaque, hung round their neck with the letters (WN), then at the end of the day, would be caned by the headmaster"
Pleading my innocence I said;
"Its was not actually me, who did this terrible thing"
David *"grump"* never one to mince his words and always ready to defend his friend and colleague said;
"No it wasn't Mick Pickwick, just some English smart arse like him in from the past"
Much to the amusement of everyone present.

Thursday 1st April 2004, 8 years on, from the surprise visit to Pickwick's courtyard by David and Jerry *"with their cunning plan".* 5 years after we first became officers of the RBL club, I showed the club committee members a bank statement which had arrived that day.

It truly was a pivotal moment in the club's recent history.
The Llanrwst RBL Business Account had over £100,000 in the bank, for the first time ever.
"£100,003.63 to be precise".
Many people thought it was an *"April fools joke"*, a fake document; *"We had mocked up on the computer"*, but no, it was the original bank statement.
This *"milestone"* was the result of hard work by officers, committee members and staff over many years.
Cath Evans, our wages clerk, was nearly in tears at the news, recalling how difficult things were in the past, when the club was struggling to pay the bills and constantly worrying if the staff would get paid their wages. Sheila Thompson, who shared an office with Cath was also quite emotional and both were full of praise for everyone concerned.

There was a quiet celebration in the bar that evening. The same week, our security system, living on borrowed time, was replaced with an up-to-date piece of equipment, with many more cameras and colour monitors, one of which was positioned behind the bar, which staff and customers alike could see.
Entering the Bar, Jerry, David, Rich and Edgar were surprised to see the bar area packed, yet no one was sitting down, watching the live sport. They all seemed engrossed with the new monitor, concentrating on one live feed, rather than the 9 split screen images it can display.
A closer look revealed a couple in the closed concert room, engaged in some *"horizontal adult activity"*, right beneath a recently installed camera. David was dissuaded from throwing a bucket of water over them, to disturb their carnal activities.
He did however curtail the impromptu evening's entertainment they were providing, by shouting at the couple to leave.
Whether they had reached a satisfactory conclusion to their

activities is pure conjecture, but an undignified exit in a state of partial undress left a voyeuristic audience in the bar, extremely disappointed.

David returned to the bar, to loud disapproval and boos from all quarters, it was his turn to be: *"the villain of the piece"*.

As neither participant in today's x-rated entertainment was with their *"usual partner"*, the blackmail value of the videotape was the source of much conjecture and amusement.

The office team, Sheila, Cath and myself learned about this, the next morning, before instructing the staff to *"wipe the videotape clean"*.

Experience tells us, not all orders are followed to the letter, but hopefully on this occasion, all incriminating evidence has been destroyed.

Another busy night Man U v Liverpool.

*"Now for ten years we've been on our own,
And moss grows fat on a rolling stone"
Don McClean
"American Pie"*

Chapter 28

Mike *Marsh looking a bit Johnny Cash(ish)*

Mike and Geraint the sound engineer did a fantastic job running the Open Mic, on the first Friday of every month. Mike has now been struck down with Parkinson's Disease,(2024). It's a cruel blow for a musician, when they can no longer play the guitar or act as the MC, which he did with distinction.
We wish him well for the future.

The RBL branch has been under new management now for 12 months. We meet quarterly as a committee, unlike the club which gathers monthly. Edgar the branch chairman and myself as secretary attend regional meetings which take place all over North Wales.

Llanrwst RBL's recruitment success has seen it become the second largest branch in North Wales, after Flint, passing Colwyn Bay and Llandudno in the process.

Llanrwst hosted its first regional meeting for many years, where we discussed the anniversary of *"Victory in Japan"*, 60 years ago. While V J Day was still 18 months away Llanrwst branch had decided to organise a celebration involving 150 pensioners on the town square.

There will be lots of events to mark the occasion, with Llanrwst central to its success. The practice of holding the regional RBL meetings on Saturdays suited most of the other branch officials who were retired. It did not suit Edgar and I who were still working.

We had some success with alternating this on occasions, Sunday mornings being the preference for us.

North Wales is very spread out geographically. So a meeting in Holyhead, Anglesey if travelling from Wrexham is a round trip of nearly 200 miles.

Llanrwst is in the centre of North Wales, it is also nearer to where the majority of members reside, so we lobbied for the meeting to be in the Conwy County region, with Llanrwst club happy to be the venue on a regular basis. There was some limited success, with this because the more central the meeting, the better the attendance figures appeared to be.

What we were unable to do was make the meetings interesting. Despite the good intentions of those attending, other than poppy appeal information, they were a chore, two hours of sheer purgatory, 4 times a year.

At every Llanrwst branch meeting, Edgar and I bigged up the regional meetings with their feast of food, free drinks and dancing girls, hoping replacements could share this onerous pleasure with us, but to no avail.

No other committee member could be tempted to volunteer or were prepared to relieve Edgar or myself for even for one meeting, unsurprisingly.

Coach trips for members, has a long tradition at the Llanrwst Royal British Legion, although, they had fallen out of favour, before our tenure. Perhaps the predictability of always, having a mystery tour to Rhyl, contributed to its demise.

We were asked to revive this, so over the next few years, we organised a number of day trips. One of these trips was a visit to the RAF Museum Cosford.

It started with a fully booked 52 seater coach starting from the Cenotaph, Llanrwst at 8.30 am. Having to feed 52 members with several meals during the day, meant that arrival times had to be strictly adhered to, for the day to run smoothly. First stop for breakfast was at the Ponderosa, Horseshoe Pass, near Llangollen, before going on to RAF Museum Cosford, near Shrewsbury.

Most said they enjoyed their visit, my lasting memory was seeing the only Japanese Yokosuuka MXY7, rocket powered suicide plane in the UK. It was the smallest aircraft in the exhibition, technically not really a plane, but a flying bomb.

The Kamikaze pilots (mostly under 25 years old) were trained to have one mission, blowing up enemy ships. There were 2600 kamikaze suicide attacks, which killed over 7000 allied naval personnel. Some Kamikaze pilots returned, which brought dishonour to their families. They may have missed the target, or were unable to find an enemy ship.

For obvious reasons, no one was trained to return to base or land an aircraft. This left some difficult questions for survivors to answer after the war, yes some returned home.

"*What did you do in the war dad?*"

"*I was a kamikaze suicide pilot, son*".

Leaving the Museum we went to a Pub in Oswestry for Dinner. The final stop was at Chirk Royal British Legion for a few drinks. There were a number of free games of bingo for those interested, or you could just chill. We then returned to the RBL club in Llanrwst.

In 2004 it cost £10 a ticket for the day, this coved the coach and all meals and £5 spending money Most members got great enjoyment from these outings, however there was one regular lady participant, who moaned that;

"*she could not get on the bus first*",

Then further complained;

"*the spending money each received was inadequate*",

This was before we had even set off.

She made the mistake of getting on David's coach where she continued her tirade:

"*Queuing for breakfast was not for her*",

"*neither was the consistency of her egg yolk up to scratch, during breakfast*".

"*Dinner was also not to her liking*" and

"*the bingo was fixed*".

Before boarding the coach home David said;

"One more word out of you and you're walking home and don't you even think of putting your name down, for a coach trip again"

The next year, she took the hint and excused herself from the excursion.

The elderly lady who for years sat next to her on these forays, was asked if she missed her friend? It turned out she had

nothing but praise for David saying;
"No more fxxxxxx moaning Minnie ever again, thank heaven"

There were several visits to Cosford, one which took in the British Ironworks Centre and Shrewsbury. This trip had three coachloads of members, which made it a logistical nightmare to organise, particularly finding places to feed that amount of people.

"Mr president", Ken Davies, a coach marshal for the day, famously refused to board one of the coaches.

Ken, in his early seventies at the time, claimed the coach driver was old enough to be his father and refused to set foot on the coach. He got his wish, being replaced by Jerry, who joined Big Rich for the trip as co-marshall.

Ken's former nonagenarian driver, then had a brake failure on the Horseshoe Pass, Llangollen, with smoke billowing everywhere before managing to stop, leaving two very unhappy marshal's, Rich and Jerry to sort it out.

Their day was not helped by the sight of Ken Davies, waving and laughing at them as he passed them totally unsympathetic to their plight.

There were several visits to the National Arboretum, near Burton on Trent, Staffordshire which were very popular, as were excursions to Liverpool on a few occasions. The best feedback came from Port Sunlight on the Wirral, where we employed a guide, who explained the history of the site and the Lady Lever gallery.

Chapter 29

Memorable for the wrong reasons, was a bizarre trip to Rhyl. Whose fault it was I cannot recall, but the buffet organised at a well known club was insufficient for the size of our party.
So,10 of us, mostly committee members, went to the local "spoons" to eat. To make things easier everyone ordered a mixed grill. We were all served a plateful of burnt black food. It was almost impossible to distinguish any of the food. I took mine back, explaining;
"All the meals are burnt to a crisp, so could you please issue refunds for everyone."
The very young person serving me refused, claiming;
"there was nothing wrong with the food,"
before disappearing back into the kitchen.
He returned with four kitchen staff, one with a cleaver, others armed with spatulas and other kitchen tools, who rushed out of the kitchen towards me.
David, Big Rich, Colin and others, are no *"shrinking violets"* and were on their feet in a flash, one look at them and the staff's bravado quickly dissipated as;
"discretion became the better part of valour"
As they hastily fled back into the kitchen .
A Junior manager appeared, apologised and refunded the money. On leaving we noticed Rich had eaten his meal, we all stared at him in utter amazement.
"Get over yourselves, I've eaten much worse, you pussies"
he bellowed.

We seem to have gained a reputation for courting controversy. There may be some justification for those holding this view, but trouble does have a habit of following us at times, often without any provocation on our part.

Baroness Christine Humphreys is a case in point, her comments about the club and its officials were totally unprovoked, ill informed and unjustified.

If we were mean spirited, we would point out;

Christine was voted an (AM) Assembly Member (we use the word elected, metaphorically) despite only receiving 12% of the vote in the constituency.

She finished fourth in the North Wales election behind Labour, Conservative and Plaid Cymru in 1999. In the real world that's a failure, here in Wales you can finish last, but still get awarded a seat on a regional list, which is what happened to the Liberal candidate Christine. Christine's *"victory"* (for want of a better word) became a springboard to another unelected position as a Liberal Baroness, chosen by other non elected people like herself.

So despite being rejected by 88% of the North Wales electorate, she joins over 800 peers elevated to the House of Lords, receiving £342 a day, (Who can claim £100 overnight allowance). The £50,000 a year in allowances, they can claim each year is also free from tax.

Compare that to the *"Personal Tax Threshold of £12500"*, the rest of us start paying tax on. This freezing of tax thresholds till 2027 was approved by the House of Lords following the last Tory Budget before the general Election in July 2024.

As the Old Etonian, PM, Lord Cameron famously said;
"We're all in this together"

Not being mean spirited, we are not going to mention any of these things about our " *Ermine clad local Peeress* ".

Llanrwst football teams past and present.

The Llanrwst football team is a great asset to the town and Clwb Llanrwst is honoured to sponsor them.

Chapter 30

Christmas staff parties, where committee members and staff get together, were also the norm in the past. There would be a meal and a disco lasting a few hours. The one night of the year, when we were all off duty and could relax and let our hair down.
On one of these occasions, David, completely out of character suggested to me;
"we dress up and do a turn".
We wigged up and dressed as hippies to sing,
"I Got you Babe " as Sonny and Cher,
David being Sonny of course, to my Cher.
Today it would be all over Facebook, then, not even an embarrassing photo.
Christmas, these days, the staff go for a meal and a night out amongst themselves, perhaps they see their employers enough times during the year, and deserve a break from us.
There's a kids Halloween party each year and a Christmas party for children, which we have never restricted to just member's offspring.
Three distinguished Santa Claus's over the years were the late Cyril Roberts, former doorman, Tank Williams and Malcolm (*Cheese boy*) Owen.
In 2005 the club had 1049 members, our highest figure to date. A successful lottery application by the branch, towards VJ Day, (Victory in Japan Day) meant we could buy trestle tables, hire chairs and have money left over for a banquet, including wine, for the occasion. It was the biggest event in RBL Llanrwst's history with a street party for 150 on Ancaster square, opposite the club.
15 Members from Llanfaelog, RBL Branch, Anglesey asked if they could join us for the day, so we made them our guests of honour, including them in all the planned entertainment.

The weather was perfect for the occasion. The pensioner members were waited on by committee members and there was live music throughout the day. 12 women members dressed in WW2 uniforms added to the mood and kept the guests entertained.

A Disco with 1940's themed music followed later, in the club. There was widespread press coverage of the event, attended by town and county councillors. A poppy collection on the day raised £447

Continuing the good news, we received a letter from Crossfield House, a RBL home for disabled ex service personnel, thanking the Llanrwst branch, for supplying them with 6 new portable televisions. The money was raised by holding sponsored walks and various other events over the last 12 months.

Good news never comes in "threes"; so not unexpectedly, a recurring problem surfaced.

At the next branch meeting, a former committee member's letter arrived, recycling the false information about my plans to change the RBL to a Labour club.

Extract from 2005 branch minutes;

The Secretary M Bucknall said; "*If I had any aspirations, to change the RBL to a labour club, I would have supported the previous committee, who nearly bankrupted the club, making a takeover more likely, with its poor economic record. Only failed RBL clubs are susceptible to hostile takeovers*"

2006 was a record breaking year for the club, sales increased, membership stabilised at over 1000 members. The benevolent fund paid out £10,000 to worthy causes, which included many sports groups, local organisations and charities.

The annual club accounts for 2006 showed a bank balance of £149,027.

The finance committee of David, Jerry and myself, made an

appointment with HSBC to meet their new regional financial consultant.

The last time we had gathered together, inside this bank was 7 years ago in 1999, when the club was heavily in debt. That day you may recall we were told;

"We were not an economic proposition", having failed to answer a single question positively, during a failed loan application.

Our previous banking experience had the manager displaying an autocratic and superior attitude, clearly wishing he was somewhere else. He was certainly pleased to see the back of us that day, preferring perhaps his local Freemasonry get together.

The welcome we received was in total contrast to our earlier experience, today we were *"treasured business associates"* and *"trusted commercial partners"*.

There was no hasty departure on this occasion, time was of no consequence and our hosts demeanour, was charming, sympathetic, and obliging.

Having done some research, we asked about no-risk investment opportunities, linked to the stock exchange, aware that under current banking legislation the first £85,000 of investment is protected. These schemes that we had researched, were oversubscribed, and not available any more, but he would contact us again should a similar opportunity arise.

The next year, the consultant contacted us about a new stock market tracker scheme lasting for three years. We duly invested £85,000 in the scheme.

We were able to follow the progress of the investment, in the financial press and online.

The stock market success during this period produced a return of £14,000 for the club. This allowed the club to forgo an annual increase in beer prices, despite higher costs and rising brewery bills. Similar investments have continued to the present day.

Llanrwst British Legion F C 1973/74

Tony Wellings Mel Parry Robert Hughes Brian Thomas Rob Geldart Mally Roberts
Jerry Thomas Ivor Kendall Terry Thomas Gerald Pierce Malcolm Spencer Colin Pierce Tony Brown
Jimmy Sweeney Peris Parry John Powell David Mogsy Williams

We have had the past and present teams, now we are going back even further, 50 years in fact. Jerry Thomas, a mere 28 years old here, far left middle row, the centre half for the RBL team. His brother Terry is to the right of the Manager, Gerald Pierce a former international goalkeeper who played amateur football for Wales

Chapter 31

30 years ago Saturday nights were busy with the concert room often full. Groups like *"Pink Cadillac"* would perform, with enough bar takings to justify the cost of these expensive bands.
Equally Christmas and New Year were packed when live acts provided the entertainment.
Over the years the interest declined, more members celebrated the festive period at home with their families. It became uneconomic to have live acts, with such small audiences on Saturday night and Bank Holidays.
One evening, two couples in the bar approached Jerry and I, reminiscing about the great entertainment the club laid on in those halcyon days, telling us about their favourite local band.
We explained the financial difficulties and lack of support today for this type of event, but against our better judgement, agreed to book their preferred band, hoping to be proved wrong, with a well attended evening of music.
Despite widespread publicity there was barely anyone in attendance on the night. We felt sorry for the band, playing to an empty room, with no atmosphere.
In the bar Jerry and I spot the two couples, whose favourite band, which they requested, was playing live in the concert room, while they are sitting in the bar.
When asked sarcastically by Jerry;
"Why aren't you in the concert room supporting your favourite band, now playing to an empty room?"
They replied;
"They could not be bothered going down to see them"
It's days like these, when you wonder, why you bother, but there's *"no pleasing some folk"*.
Football both internationally and at Premiership level have grown in popularity. The Wales football team's recent success along

with Sky TV football coverage has also attracted a different and more diverse audience. Gone are the old televisions, replaced by four large screens and improved sound systems. Sport now is the main entertainment in the club, despite the Sky and TNT subscriptions being expensive. The cost can be justified however, because it's still lucrative, attracting very large audiences, during the football season. Clwb Llanrwst has become the most popular venue for live sport in the local area. Another change over the years allows members to book the concert room at no cost, for birthdays, anniversaries or other notable occasions. They provide their own entertainment, with or without food. These arrangements are more cost effective for the business providing enough attend and the bar takings, cover heating, lighting and bar staff for the event.

Ten years after David and Jerry's first "*Pickwick's courtyard encounter*", we are still asked what drew the three of us together?
Not sure any of us can fully answer that question, but there are some personality crossovers. We're all stubborn, argumentative and have anti-establishment tendencies, none of which are ideal characteristic traits for creating harmony, or working successfully as a team..
It's organised chaos at times, but somehow we find consensus and arrive at decisions, which in the majority of cases, find favour with the rest of our committee colleagues.
None of us are suited to the RBL branch ethos, we are happy doing the Poppy Appeal, and Armistice, but have problems with the armed services strict bureaucracy, where orders must be obeyed.
The RBL organisation, not surprisingly also has real difficulties dealing with us, the so called "*awkward squad*" who:
"*question orders, stretch the rules and argue back*"

These factors seem to apply to all of us, but if you add *"nuisance"* to these traits, my friends and family might concur; *"That's me to a Tee*

On August the 25th 1949, my mother Ada, travelling from Knighton, on the Welsh border to Coventry, had to stop the train at Solihull, so that I could be born in the local hospital.*(no that does not make me a brummie)*

I am forever reminded of the fact:

"I was a nuisance even before I was born"

When I was 12 years old I recorded an unusually high mark in Religious Instruction (RI). This led to an invitation to the opening of Coventry Cathedral on April 23rd 1962 which was also attended by Queen Elizabeth.

Finding the whole occasion, nothing more than a display of opulence for the rich and privileged, I had an epiphany moment, becoming an atheist that very day.

At Nicholas Chamberlain school, Bedworth, nr Nuneaton I refused to attend the religious morning assembly or do RI lessons since losing my faith. Out of over 1000 pupils at the school, there were three who opted out, a Plymouth Brethren, a Sikh, and an atheist, all of us were excused from all religious lessons and morning assemblies.

I could not help being a *"nuisance"* before I was born, but understand that's no excuse for remaining a *"nuisance"* at school, throughout my trade union career and continuing this for three decades, while serving in a number of capacities in Llanrwst club.

A 24 hour snooker marathon for charity in 1996 at the Llanrwst Royal British Legion club, describing us as "top local potters", which describes John (Baldy) Roberts, third from the right, but greatly overstates the snooker ability of most of us.

VALLEY ACES CUE IN FOR A MARATHON

☐ The Llanrwst Pavilion Fund was given a boost this week when a group of top local 'potters' took part in a 24-hour fundraising 'snookerthon'. The event, at the Royal British Legion Club, in Llanrwst, raised over £140 on the night - £38 of which was donated by the players themselves from a 10 pence penalty for each fowl they imposed.
More money is expected from individual sponsorships.

Recent celebrations for Clwb Llanrwst Pool team lifting the cup in 2023/24

Chapter 32

While on holiday with Gill at Lyme Regis, Dorset during May 2007, I found myself unusually short of breath, when tackling the shortest of hills There had been a virus going around, which caused respiratory problems, so I was not too concerned.
On getting home I had a few check ups but the problem persisted.
My doctor eventually sent me to Bangor hospital for an x-ray, which failed to indicate what the problem was.
The radiologist, said;
"it's not my field, but you should ask your doctor for an angiogram, but don't say I said so"
My doctor advised against, saying;
" they are not without risk",
but reluctantly agreed to send me anyway.
They do 10 angiograms at a time at Glan Clwyd, Rhyl, which involves putting dye in your arteries to check your blood flow. Following these tests, the consultant discusses the results with you.
The other 9 patients are opposite and adjacent to you, with only curtains between, so you can hear every word the doctor says to the other patients. Conversations all seemed to follow a similar pattern;
"Mrs Jones, we can do nothing until your weight is stabilised."
"Mr Griffiths, until we get your diabetes under control, an operation is out of the question"
"Miss Williams It's too dangerous to operate with your blood pressure so high"
The other 6 were all given similar advice, meaning there would be no operations. I was last in line and the doctor, with great enthusiasm bellowed;
"Mr Bucknall fantastic news, I have never seen anyone, in better

condition than you, to have a triple bypass"
Gill and I were stunned, I asked him to repeat this, not sure that *"fantastic"* and *"triple bypass"* can be used in the same sentence. Smiling broadly, still much enthused, he confirmed his diagnosis.
"What are the alternatives?" I asked
"Without an operation, trying to breath, would put a strain on your heart, leading to a coronary and eventually death." the doctor happily quipped.
"Not much of an option then" I said
Not long afterwards on Friday,13th July, Edgar Parry drove Gill and I to the Royal Hospital, Manchester for my operation the next day. Following the triple bypass, being a lousy patient,
"or more likely cementing my credentials as a bloody nuisance again"
I was demanding to go home within a few days
After passing a few tests, I was reluctantly discharged on Tuesday, 3 days after the operation.
The district nurse visited a few days later to remove my stitches. After the nurse left, David, Richard and Jerry arrived to visit the patient at Pickwick's, without showing the slightest sympathy for my plight. Richard compared me to a well known benefit fraudster who had never worked in his life, while David said;
"Get over yourself, you lazy Bxxxxxx".
They then devoured my grapes and chocolates, before Jerry demanded that I;
"Stop feeling sorry for yourself, and get back in the office, as your in-tray demands urgent attention"

Chapter 33

In 2008 The chairman of the RBL County committee rang to inform me the application for gold badges in recognition of the work done by Ken Davies and Edgar Parry had been rejected. He didn't think Ken, a committee member, president and standard bearer for nearly 40 years warranted recognition, notwithstanding his attendance at 100's of ceremonial events and funerals for ex-service members, as an RBL Standard Bearer.

He was also a designated poppy seller over the same period. Equally Edgar has held office, on club and branch committees for over 20 years including 10 years as the current chairman of club and branch. Like Ken he has worked his socks off selling poppies house to house and in the local supermarket.

The RBL journal reported that gold badges in other districts were awarded to people with very little service and in our opinion without real merit.

We pointed out that Llanrwst, with a population of 3000, has 1000 RBL members, which was quite unique for such a small catchment area. We also collected £8000 for the poppy appeal last year which is unmatched by any similar size town in North Wales. Ken and Edgar are key figures in membership recruitment, Armistice and the Poppy Appeal

These are the first applications for gold badges by the Llanrwst RBL branch for 15 years. Llanrwst branch officers in the past, were awarded gold badges, some were no doubt deserved, others were far less worthy than Ken and Edgar.

We found the organisers comments condescending when justifying his decision by claiming;

"*He knows best*" and

"*perhaps I could have another look at it in the future*"

We also reminded him of our attempts, to get an investigation into the mismanagement of the branch and club at RBL Llanrwst, which he and his fellow officers refused to support.

Perhaps the-powers-that-be were disappointed that the *"Llanrwst dissidents"* were exonerated and received an apology from national officials which reflected badly on the North Wales administration.
The senior official then went on the offensive, criticising Edgar and I for not attending all county meetings.
We pointed out, we have to take a day off from our businesses to attend quarterly meetings, which are the most mind-numbing, boring, soul-destroying events you can imagine.
We further reminded him that our RBL branch predecessors, who the senior officers seemed to prefer working with, were able to break the rules with impunity, having no AGM for years, while spending the proceeds from a gaming machine, which they turned a blind eye to.
It became very clear, my championing the merits of my colleagues, for gold badges was not helping their cause. We had caused a lot of embarrassment at regional level, so Llanrwst officers would not reap the rewards their achievements deserved.
NB *"Some years later both Ken and Edgar gained the recognition they both deserved, with Gold Badges."*

On a brighter note, Bass, our brewery supplier, informed us that the club's increased sales were the largest amongst its clubs and pubs in the UK during the last 12 months.
This achievement came with a UK national award and a prize of an all inclusive holiday for two in Lanzarote.
The club committee discussed who should get the prize.
We came up with a number of current officers and staff, who have excelled in their duties for the club.

Eventually though the committee decided the fairest way was to put every member's name in a hat and draw out a winner, which gave everyone an equal chance of winning.

You won't be surprised, no committee members or their families won the prize, but a lovely couple did and thoroughly enjoyed their unexpected holiday.

Unknown to us this was a precursor to even greater recognition later.

David (grump) came up with the idea of a Lotto, where you pick 3 numbers, pay a £1 and if they match the national lottery numbers, you win the kitty. Every penny is paid out and the kitty increases each week if the numbers are not matched.

Over £6000 was paid out on one occasion.

Bemoaning his luck Jerry "bach" missed this large payout, when winning it the following week, taking home just over £200.

The benefit for the club is the 200+ participants come to the club to pay their stake each week, while there, some may partake of a drink or two.

It's also a useful recruitment tool, as only members can participate. It is still as popular today, 15 years later.

One winter, there was a terrible smell in the club, members were walking out, it seemed the drains were blocked. Several hours of investigation could not find the cause, making the middle room a no go area.

It transpired that Ianto Thomas had purchased a pork joint a few days earlier, hung it on the coat rail under a jacket, above a hot radiator. He then went home and forgot all about it.

Two days later It had become rancid, luckily David who has no sense of smell was able to remove the rotten meat, rather than evacuate the premises.

The word went out, we could not have a repeat of this health hazard and Ianto would have to *"become a vegetarian"* if he wants to retain his membership.

On hearing this, Ianto, waving his walking stick, accosted me in Pickwick's, red in the face with fury. He hurled insults and profanities at me for several minutes, to the surprise of a group of genteel ladies enjoying their afternoon teas.

It then suddenly dawned on him, he had been set up, when seeing me; *"pretending to be an angler reeling in a catch"*.

He took it very well and roared with laughter, to the utter amazement of my customers.

With a twinkle in his eye, he went round all the ladies apologising, before removing his hat and bowing to universal applause, as he departed.

Ianto is no longer with us, but will always be remembered fondly as a great Llanrwst character and a true club legend.

More recent success for the Club pool team

> "Ain't got no time for the corner boys
> down on the street makin' all that noise"
> Bruce Springsteen.
> " Jersey girl"
> Written by "Tom Waits"

Chapter 34

One year on, since the smoking ban, (2007) we have seen a slight decline in members, but the competitive pricing policy meant we had as many active members, amongst the 950 we recruited.

An appeal against the club's rateable value, based on projected losses due to the smoking ban, proved to be successful.

This again improved the clubs finances as the Sky and BT account is based on the rateable value of the building.

Being placed in a lower banding also reduced the actual business rates bill.

Forever switching energy suppliers and trying to keep the service contracts at a reasonable level all made marginal gains and helped keep the club competitive.

Looking at the high cost of our building insurance, we sought some cheaper quotes. Contacting RBL Head office I was informed building insurance was done collectively, covering all RBL buildings in their portfolio, after which, we pay a share. They said;

"You cannot insure RBL owned building, yourself individually."

The RBL estates department could not explain how a policy covering hundreds of buildings, cost twice as much as that we negotiated for a single building.

They seemed very upset when being told;

"*Surely anyone with a modicum of negotiating skills, should be able to do a better job than this*".
The problem is they (*the Owners*) are not paying the bills, we (*the tenant*) are, so there is no incentive for them to get a better deal.
The manager of the estates department at the time was Robin Mann. The unflattering surname pseudonym, David gave him started with "B" which rhymes with "plastered",
meant he was forever known as the "robbin' bxxxxxx"

During Christmas 2009 David *"grump"*, completely out of character, has made an enormous punch, heavily alcoholic, festooned with floating fresh fruit and it's free to everyone.
Jerry asks him;
"If he's had a visit from the ghost of Christmas present, having abandoned his lifetime Scrooge principles, now giving stuff away free in the club"
The New Year arrives and as it's a quiet month, the club rewards its stalwart customers with a reduction of beer prices, each weekend during January. Running for 4 years now It's greatly appreciated and does bring in more custom.
David has discovered there are 5 weekends in January 2009 and is berating the fact, It will therefore cost more to subsidise the beer reduction. He reverts to type, abandoning his;
"Ghost of Christmas present persona"
With the debate turning into a bizarre Monty Pythonesque sketch, David says;
"We can't have 15 cheap days in a month"
I said " *What do you want us to do, have our own Llanrwst calendar which only has 28 days in January"*.
David said "*that's just stupid*".
Jerry retorts;
*"Llanrwst has its our own flag, Cymru, Lloegr a Llanrwst (Wales,

England and Llanrwst) and once applied to the UN to become an independent micronation. If we can have our own flag and become a nation, it should be no problem having our own unique calendar".

Big Rich shaking his head, while listening to this said;
"It's the first day of the New Year. Do I have to listen to another 364 days of this shite"

We think David's punch was responsible for this foolishness and we all hope he ditches this *"un-David-like"* version of himself and reverts back to his normal *"Scrooge"* persona again next year.
"Put a punch on by all means, but make them pay for it. That's the David we know and love."

The club is still doing very well, although things are still difficult with the branch. Edgar and I try to attend all the quarterly regional meetings but nothing very interesting happens in the main. There is no discussion about Royal British Legion clubs, they are never an agenda item.

Everything revolves around the welfare issues, which of course are their primary role, but clubs are important too, there is no regional or national forum for clubs, who are very much left to their own devices. There are no training courses in how to run a licensed business. The RBL Head office does not even provide a manual for committees, advising on best practices.

Out of the other 30 representatives attending regional branch meetings, none have roles in clubs. The other thing they have in common is everyone is above retirement age, with the exception of the paid RBL officers in attendance.

It is blindingly obvious, in the next few years, most branches will close as younger people shy away from an outdated institution. An expensive market survey concluded;
"modernisation was the way forward" and we understand several million pounds have been earmarked, for a radical change in

direction.

Introducing City/ large town RBL hubs, into shopping centres which will open and recruit members on the high streets, is their big idea.

We have suggested they could spend this money, more wisely, by investing in the RBL clubs which are closing all over the UK. While Llanrwst RBL is in no danger of closing now, it still needs £150,000 spent on the building, a property that the RBL estates department owns but refuses to invest in.

It has buildings all over Wales, but does not spend a penny on their upkeep. The clubs have been the best recruitment tool the organisation has, they are an asset, but there are no strategic plans regarding their future.

If a club the size of Llanrwst RBL closes, the £15000 subscriptions paid directly to the RBL head-office in 2009 would be lost.(RBL subscriptions in 2024 would equate to £32,000) Very few, if any members, maintain their branch membership, once their club closes. Letting clubs close, then selling the building off, may not be the official corporate policy of RBL, but that's the rudderless direction of travel the organisation is heading.

"The City RBL hubs, were as we expected, a total failure and a complete waste of money, as we and many others predicted"

Chapter 35

Having had my head shaved for Charity, by Big Rich and my son Nathan, in Pickwick's courtyard, raising over £900, I thought my good deeds were over for the year.

It was not to be, Gary Michael, Ken Davies' son, and I took on the challenge of walking from Ross on Sea to Rhyl for the Poppy Appeal, during early autumn.

Fully recovered from the triple bypass, with a number of training days behind us, we decided to set a fast pace, bearing in mind Gary is 25 years or so younger than me.

There were hundreds of groups taking part, including some from the armed services. We worked ourselves through the field arriving at Rhyl, having completed the 13.5 miles in around 3 hours.

There was supposed to be a contingent of Royal British Legion dignitaries, a brass band and the Mayor of Ross on Sea to welcome us. Not only was there no one to greet us, the absence of a finishing line left us somewhat confused.

30 minutes later we noticed the finishing tape was being put up, ready for the arrival of the walkers.

So we watched from the sidelines, as the remaining contestants crossed the finishing line, greeted by the Major, who dished out medals, with the proceedings recorded for posterity by an official photographer.

We clapped them home, along with the newly formed crowds, accompanied by a quickly assembled brass band.

While being denied our moment of glory today, we were content, knowing we had pushed the poppy appeal up to record levels.

The Club's Annual accounts for 2008, published in 2009 show £146,459, in the business account, so despite the smoking ban, the club continued to prosper. The Poppy appeal again exceeded £8,000, helped by the walk and some other fundraising events.

We cannot report everything associated with the poppy appeal went smoothly. Boots, who had recently taken over as the main chemist in town, refused to display a poppy appeal box.

We thought it was just a rogue manager being awkward, but no it seemed to be Boot's official policy.

Boots is owned by Walgreens Boots Alliance, a multinational US company. Ken Jenkins the Poppy Appeal organiser ensured that the press knew about this policy and the company received some unwelcome journalistic approaches, on the subject.

Threats of a boycott by RBL members and other Llanrwst townspeople over this issue, kept the issue alive.

We can now report that Boots is fully supportive of the Poppy Appeal, we have all moved on, as they say, with this little hiccup behind us.

Our caterers who provide the buffet for Armistice were double booked in 2008, leaving us with a last minute problem to resolve.

Unable to find a replacement caterer on this occasion, Gill and I laid on a buffet for 150 on Armistice Sunday, from Pickwick's kitchen designed for about 30 covers. This meant a 5.00 am start, with our daughters Jemma and Danielle roped in to give us a hand, and son Nathan detailed to deliver the buffet to the club. This was one of many Armistice buffets we did in the intervening years.

RBL Llanrwst, presumably run by a rogue "dissident group" are in the headlines again, not for embarrassing a multinational company, or being wrongly criticised by a member of the House of Lords. No strange as it may seem, We are being praised and celebrated.

Headline; Weekly News December 3rd 2009.

"LLANRWST CLUB WINS PRESTIGIOUS AWARD"

The Prestigious award ceremony which took place at the Palace Hotel Manchester last Friday November 27th is the highest accolade for hundreds of clubs across the UK.

Llanrwst British Legion was surprised to learn they were amongst the finalists for best community club and best club Committee awards. There were golf, tennis, amateur and professional football clubs, many cricket and working-mens clubs along with works clubs from the private and public sector present.

Llanrwst with a population of approx 3000 and a club membership of 1000 was up against finalists;

BBC London club, Bury football club and a Health Service trust, all of which dwarfed the RBL Llanrwst in resources and membership"

The tension heightened as the envelope for best committee was finally opened by television presenter Claire Balding who declared;

"Llanrwst Royal British Legion club committee the Winner"

Edgar Parry and I received the award to rapturous applause.

Mr Parry, Club chairman said;

"It was the culmination of 10 years of work by the Llanrwst RBL Committee. Those committee members not here tonight notably David Hughes and Jerry Thomas deserve a special mention, along with its dedicated staff and the continuing support of its members, which has seen the club transformed from a debt ridden club in 1999 to where we are today a decade later. Good financial management, particularly by my colleague here

today, Mr Bucknall who was treasurer for the first 4 years, steering the club through the financial crisis we inherited, before becoming club secretary in 2003. This award also recognised the charitable and social contributions made to the local community. During the past 12 months the Llanrwst RBL club social fund has donated £10,000 to good causes..
It also raised £8000 for the Poppy appeal"
The Weekly news reporter Samantha Castle closed the story with;
"The secretary said the award was a real David and Goliath moment and while it was a surprise it was well deserved. Membership is growing, which bucks the trend in the industry, with 100 new members joining since October.
Particularly pleasing is, many youngsters are joining the club, which is essential for the viability of the club going forward."

Extract from Club Mirror 2009

A Legion club in North Wales has triumphed at the 2009 Club Mirror Awards.

Llanrwst received the award for best Club Committee at the annual ceremony, which recognises excellence in Britain's club industry. The ceremony took place in Manchester on 25 November, and was hosted by BBC sports presenter Clare Balding.

Llanrwst's prize was collected by Club Secretary Michael Bucknall and Chairman Edgar Parry (pictured with Clare). In his acceptance speech, Mr Parry said: "Winning the award was the culmination of 10 years' hard work by the Llanrwst Committee, its dedicated staff and the continuing support of its members, which has seen good financial management allow us to survive through some difficult times and for our membership to grow." Despite tough economic conditions, the club welcomed more than 100 new members through its doors last year.

Gary Michael and I waiting for the Mayor, the brass band and other walkers to arrive after completing the charity walk

Bobby Dean   "Burgess"
Two great Llanrwst Club Characters, It's an absolute pleasure to have known them both.

Chapter 36

The next year organisers of the Club Mirror Awards rang the club, suggesting a visit to Llanrwst, for a follow up article on the winners of "best committee."
We were happy to oblige, so extended an open invitation to the Club Mirror representatives.
They further suggested:
"*I should allow my name to go forward as a candidate for best secretary at the 2010 awards*".
Without hesitation I refused explaining,
"*It would damage the team ethic, we have built up over many years, singling out individuals for praise.*
The best *"committee award"* was for the whole team and after last year's win, we had a little celebratory drink, a few taps on the back, then got back to running the club again
The visit by Club Mirror representatives must have left a good impression on them, because before leaving they said;
"We would be perfect candidates for; the Community club of the year award, having looked at the clubs social fund activity in the local area". This category is one of the most sought after awards at the 2010 ceremony. After consulting the committee we agreed to be nominated. Some weeks later we learned we had made the shortlist, so Edgar and I had another trip to Manchester to organise.
Referring earlier to *"events"* and how Llanrwst management responded to them, may have given the impression, decision making was a harmonious and straightforward procedure.
Often that's true, at other times it could be fractious.
David grump and Jerry Bach are by nature outspoken and don't suffer fools easily, so getting unanimity between the three of us on how we deal with *"events"* was far from straight forward.
When we disagreed the arguments were fierce at times. Only

once, in our 14 year relationship have I said;
"We must do this or else"
The *"else"* being left in the air but the finality was understood. That was as treasurer in 1999, proposing we reduce beer prices, despite the club being heavily in debt at the start of our tenure and only having a 2p advantage on pubs at the time. It was a risk, but a calculated one, given the parallel talks with the brewery at the time, on reducing our bills.

On most occasions, David and Jerry preferred building up capital for a rainy day. I often cautioned against this because having too much capital in the bank threatened our charitable status, as a *"not for profit organisation"*.

So on this and other issues, my finance committee colleague's views often gained the ascendancy over my minority view. These differences were never aired in public or at the committee meetings, once a decision was made; *"we all owned it"*.

Arriving in Manchester for the 2010 Club Mirror awards, Edgar and I knew we would finish in the top three for;
"The Community club of the year", having been shortlisted already, but where we would finish on the night, was still unknown.

Sheila and David wished us well, before we starting out, reminding us that, in the last few years, we have won;
"the Bass award" for most improved sales, been nominated for; *"4 Club Mirror categories"*, won *"best committee in the UK"*, turned down the nomination for *"Secretary of the year"* and will be amongst the; *"best three community UK clubs"*, regardless of the result tonight.

Edgar and I were happy wherever we finished, even finishing third gave us the honour of being the best;
"Community Club of the Year in Wales", an honour in itself.

The Master of Ceremonies for the awards presentation, opened the envelope for our category announcing, third place went to

Pennington Sports and Social club, with Beverley Golf Club being announced as runner up.
Edgar whispered in my ear:
"Have we won, they have not mentioned us yet?"
I said *"I will not believe it till they announce the winner officially,"* as I kept my fingers tightly crossed behind my back.
After a long pause, Llanrwst RBL club were finally declared the; "*UK Community club of the year*" and we made our way to the stage to receive the award.
It was a special night for Wales, as Colwyn Bay Cricket Club followed our success winning the "*UK club of the year award*", Edgar phoned through the result to the club, so we celebrated in Manchester with our friends from Colwyn Bay, while similar scenes took place in our little club in North Wales.

48 years earlier Ken Davies is having a party

Ken Davies looking like Elvis and being; "a little shook up"
With his Wife Joan and friends in 1962.

A few lighter moments for committee members, staff and Batman

Two cttee members Neil and Dave giving it; "the love"

"Stan the Man" or is it "Stan the Tran"

It's not really me, just someone "being an arse"

Batman being Batman, "as only he can"

Chapter 37

In 2011 the club was dual sourcing products, with Heineken, supplying Wrexham lager and Fosters, alongside Molsen Coors who were still our main supplier. We had been looking at costs and were concerned that wages had grown from £93,000 in 2003 to £142,000 in 2011. Cost of sales had also risen to £141,000 for the same period. This meant that Bar sales which had grown by £50,000 for the same period to £282,000 would have shown a loss without other income, which mostly came from the gaming machines.

We sat down with Coors Molsen and negotiated a new exclusive agreement, which coincided with a new brewery representative being appointed at the same time. That relationship with Molson Coors has stood the test of time, to the mutual benefit of both parties to the present day.

The club up until 2012 had 2 bar managers, restructuring saw the introduction of a General Manager for the first time, which has continued to the present day. New electric tills were also installed, as the club embarked on a modernisation program, which was long overdue.

The last few years had been relatively calm, business wise and the *"events" that* did occur, paled into insignificance compared with our earlier trials and tribulations. We now have experienced staff and senior officers with 15 years of service under their belts. So what could go wrong? Well everything as it happens, because 2013 became our;

"annus horribilis", when out of nowhere *"all hell broke loose"*
Before detailing those events, our accountants made us aware of a tax liability judgement. VAT on profits from the gaming machines, were judged illegal, which meant millions being paid back to Ladbrokes and other betting firms. Even small businesses like the club were affected by the ruling.

We claimed £27,000, in VAT back from HMRC, which we received, knowing if the Government's appeal won, we would have to pay it back.
A new tax called Gaming Machine Duty (GMD) of 20% came into effect, unsurprisingly the same rate as VAT.
That £27,000 refund became a key element in events in 2013 as does the return on the Investment of £85,000.
2013 started no differently to previous years, the minutes of the January meeting indicated the club had a good Christmas financially, membership figures were better than expected and the rest of the meeting was relatively uneventful.
"Uneventful is a highly underrated outcome, that I would recommend to any other budding club secretary."

The 2013 RBL branch AGM took place in early February, unbeknown to us, this would be the last Llanrwst branch AGM ever. In previous years, no one, other than committee members plus Stan Roberts and Bobby Dean would bother to attend. This proved to be the case again, as no names were nominated for the officer vacancies. This followed the pattern of the last 10 years, with the club committee and officers serving on the branch in the absence of any further nominations for branch officers.
A letter arrived from the Wrexham RBL district office informing the branch that;
"Officers could no longer serve as both club and branch officials."
This arrangement had been in place for 10 years following the failure to recruit branch officers in Llanrwst.
This decision made at national level threatens the very existence of the Llanrwst club.
There had been no phone calls, or any other communications about ending this agreement, prior to the letter.
Was "*St Jude, the patron saint of lost causes*" back again?.

Chapter 38

Email to RBL officer Wrexham. 8th February 2013;
I am emailing you a letter that's being posted today. I believe it's the most important letter I have ever written to the RBL.
Mick Bucknall Branch secretary
        To xxx xxxxx Wrexham office.
Yesterday 7th February 2013, Llanrwst RBL Branch had its AGM, nine of us were in attendance.
When the election of Officers came up, there were no candidates.
So the Llanrwst branch has no committee members or officers and no service committee.
This situation will not change as interest in branch activities has reached an all time low.
It should be remembered 90% of our members have never been in the services.
As Secretary of the club I have to address the implications of this decision on the future of the club and more importantly the security of employment of our staff. The club would prefer to resolve this problem, while still remaining under the umbrella of the Royal British Legion.
In the absence of a Llanrwst branch committee, there cannot be a Royal British Legion club, so serious consideration must be given to alternative arrangements which ensure the clubs continued existence.
The members of RBL Llanrwst along with the officers and committee members will not allow the club to close, so we need immediate assurances and strong leadership from the Wrexham office and the district, that they also support this position.
The district might believe that calling all the members to a meeting and warning them of the ramifications of having no

branch will encourage members to come forward and resurrect the branch.

We believe it is bound to fail, as would trying to call together former branch committee members. It has been 10 years since they last served and most were pensioners then. The fact is, they are now ex branch committee members, having done their duty over many years and want no further involvement.

During the next few days, as news spreads, I and my fellow committee members will be inundated with questions about the future of the club and its employees from members and more importantly staff.

Few will care about the demise of the branch, illustrated by the paltry AGM attendance, but they will care passionately about the future of their club. It is our belief that someone in authority with experience of dealing with similar club problems needs to come to Llanrwst and meet the club committee as a matter of urgency. We can assemble a team for any day next week ending 15th February 2013.

Prioritising the fate of the branch at the expense of the club, members and its employees, would be extremely misguided and would almost certainly lead to a collision course between the Llanrwst club and district.

Any solution has to be long term, the club cannot ever again have its future put in doubt by the action of a third party,(Llanrwst Branch) one it has no control or influence over.

Email from RBL officer 18th february 2013.
Mick I have spoken to xxxxx* and xxxxxxxx* and we can all be available to meet you in Llanrwst at 10.00 am on Tuesday March 5th. Can you confirm if this is OK with you and where we meet, (presumably the club)
**Please note xxxxx* is a senior RBL official and xxxxxxxx* is in charge of the Estates Department based in Manchester.

Chapter 39

Extract from the minutes of the Joint meeting of senior RBL officers and Llanrwst club officers held on March 5th 2013.

The Club officers expanded on the difficulties already expressed in a letter to Wrexham dated the 8th February and their disappointment on how slowly these matters were progressing. In a long discussion the committee also said they had concerns about the British Legion owning the club, but not being responsible for maintaining the building. There is over £150,000 of work required, to bring the building up to standard over the next few years.
The committee was not prepared to invest heavily in a property they did not own, reminding the senior officers the club donated the building for nothing in the past to the RBL.
In reply the club committee were told that in the absence of a branch committee, they were prepared to transfer all the members into the North Wales branch based in Wrexham. This arrangement would last a year and allow a new branch to be formed during the next 12 months.
There were other conditions including everyone being on direct debit.We rejected this short term compromise, insisting on a permanent solution that guarantees the long term future of the club
  It was agreed that District officers would again seek dispensation, for Llanrwst officers to again serve on both committees as previously agreed. The club also asked for a change in the lease arrangements or for negotiations to start, on the possibility of buying the club back from the RBL.
With answers expected next week March 11th, it was agreed that the club committee meet at the earliest opportunity to discuss

their forthcoming responses.

In closing, our visitors from Wrexham and Manchester confirmed that Llanrwst was the most successful RBL club in North Wales, with a sound financial base and a skilled management structure unmatched in the region.

An off the cuff remark during an adjournment, not missed by Jerry, David or myself, opened another can of worms.

"*RBL clubs could not buy properties from the Royal British Legion, if they are an existing tenant.*"

Several phone calls later, it was confirmed that a RBL club would have to disaffiliate its membership of the Royal British Legion to become a prospective buyer.

With the meeting coming to a close David asked one of the representatives;

"*Why did he show such little concern for the future of the club, did he think the RBL would be better off with the club closed, given the difficult relationship between the parties over the years?*"

We were all shocked by his reply:

"*If the club bought the Kings Head, the money from the sale could be put to good use, by the Royal British Legion Head office*".

There was no caveat; such as; "*It would be tragic for the town, nothing about the loss of jobs, he made it sound like the club closing, was a* win-win *situation for the RBL administration*".

This was undoubtedly "*a lightbulb moment*" and nothing would ever be the same again. That; "*off the cuff remark*" started a chain of events, with ramifications, still reverberating to the present day.

Several days later, RBL Head office rejected our request, for the club committee to continue managing the branch and referred us back to the regional committee to resolve any outstanding issues

We have now established, that some influential people at the Royal British Legion were; "*ambivalent to our fate*".
"*So where do we go from here?*"
We (David, Jerry and I) have overseen the most successful period in the clubs history, that work is still ongoing as we reorganise the managerial structure, and continue to keep the club on a strong financial footing.
Now all this is at risk again, unless we come up with a plan to save the club from closure again, 15 years after the last debacle.
We believe RBL Head office have abandoned Llanrwst club to its fate, leaving its future; "in the *lap of the gods*" while "*washing its hands*" of any responsibility.
At this stage the club committee had not considered the possibility of;
"*Starting a new club to replace the Royal British Legion club*".
"*Could this be done?*
"*Could we afford to buy the club?*"
"*Would the RBL be prepared to sell the building to us?*".
"*What would stop them selling to a developer or other interested parties?*"
We spoke to xxxxxxx, a RBL estates manager for clarification. He said;
"*Should we attempt to purchase the building, we, the tenant, could acquire preferential bidder status, which effectively means, in the first instance, they can only sell to us.*
The club would have to disaffiliate from the Royal British Legion prior to the sale."
We could not get a logical explanation why the club was unable to buy the property, without disaffiliation from the RBL.
These conditions, in our view, hasten the closure of RBL clubs and encourage them to become private clubs.

Kings Head trading as a cafe between the World Wars.
In the shadow to the far right of the photo the sign reads
Breakfasts, Luncheons, Teas, Snacks and Suppers
It was also a shop selling tobacco and confectionery.
Hanging down into the entrance is the Rotary Club sign,
so it's safe to assume the charity held its meeting
in the Kings Head. The taxi advert on the left is for
Hughes Bros Llanrwst Tel 150.

We understand it was also trading as a commercial hotel,
its main clientele being travelling salesmen. They would often
sleep 3 or more to a room, even sharing double beds with
complete strangers as they travelled from town to town.

> *"I walk a lonely road*
> *The only one that I have ever known"*
> Green Day
> *"Boulevard of broken dreams"*

Chapter 40

The club had £140,000 in the bank,(which included £14,000 from an investment and a VAT refund of £27,000).
Using informal contacts built up over many years at the RBL, we established that the asking price for buying the club would be between £100,000 and £130,000.
Our investment into the property over the years, made the building worth much more than this, especially if sold as *"a going concern"*. As a successful business we estimate the Kings Head was worth several times the likely asking price.
We let it be known that our cash reserves would stretch to a bid of £100,000.
We further learned, a locally based, business woman, *"with financial clout"* linked to the licensing trade had contacted RBL head office, attempting to buy the club.
Rumour had it;
"The plan was to close the club down"
Our "*preferential bidder status*" if we went ahead, would hopefully put a stop to that, because we could never, have matched the *"other interested party"* in a bidding process.

Email from estates department 9th April 2013 to the club secretary.
Dear mick
"I was with our valuer yesterday, who furnished me with his report on the Kings Head building. Getting straight to the point, the offer of £100,000 is considered too low, but if we can get

£110,000, my understanding is this would be acceptable".
In terms of timing I would like to get matters on the sale moving now, with an objective of having it completed by the end of August this year". xxxxxxxx

Our reply 10th April 2013;
"I have now spoken with most of the committee and all are in favour of purchasing the club at a price of £110,000.
While this won't be formally approved until tomorrow's meeting, when we have a full complement of committee members. We can be unequivocal that this transaction will happen, so let's get it done".
Mick Bucknall.

Letter to RBL district.
Dear sir
We are now in the process of purchasing the building but will also need some guidance regarding the branch.
There will be no further outgoings from the branch account, as it will be wound up, in its final year at the end of this September 2013.
The COIF fund will also need to close, this can be closed ASAP, because we no longer have the authority to apply for funds as there are no officers.
I am sure my colleagues would be happy to donate both account balances to the poppy appeal if that is allowed.
Mick Bucknall

Final letter from RBL club secretary to the district.
The continuous uncertainty the club faced, due to the failing of the branch, left the members with no real option.
Our decision to disaffiliate is the only one that provides job security for our employees and ensures that Llanrwst still has a

club, albeit not a RBL club now or for the foreseeable future.
If we are allowed, we will as promised still have a Poppy Appeal and we will organise Armistice each year with the club providing a buffet, hot drinks, crisps and pop for the children attending at the club's expense. Please convey our best wishes to the clubs, branches and officers of the RBL.
Whatever we decide to call the club in the end, it will always be referred to affectionately by many as "The Legion"
All the best Mick Bucknall

"It was also agreed a few days later, if the sale went through, the legal fees would not be the clubs responsibility, except for the conveyancing element".

The Club committee voted unanimously that the club should seek to disaffiliate from the Royal British Legion and start the process of buying the Kings Head from the Royal British Legion. There is a legal requirement to call a meeting of the full membership to endorse the committee's decision.
The meeting date was agreed and advertised in the local press as strictly members only.

A CENTENARY OF SERVICE

" They say every picture tells a story"
This one shows three happy guys who have a lot to be proud of. Between them, they have racked up over 100 years of service to the Royal British Legion and Clwb Llanrwst, serving as senior officers for both organisations .
Take you hats off to Ken Jenkins,(left) Ken Davies (centre) and Jerry Thomas (right)

Chapter 41

Special General Meeting (SGM) June 17th 2013.
The conference room was full with the officers seated on the stage. The chairman updating the membership on the failure to elect a branch committee and the consequences for the clubs future.
The offer for members to join a Wrexham branch for a year as a temporary solution, was not well received and the meeting was happy the club committee had rejected that proposal.
There was a passionate debate about the long association the club had with the Royal British Legion and the merits of disaffiliation, buying the club and becoming a private club.
Ken Davies a staunch RBL man and Standard Bearer said;
"We have to do what's right for the town, if that means becoming a private club that's what we must do."
Bobby Dean agreed with Ken and said;
"Mr Secretary you have kept your council on this, what do you think we should do?"
I replied; "Given that I have been accused on many occasions of trying to establish a Labour club to replace the RBL club, I have been reluctant to offer an opinion, which gives credence to my accusers. With that said I now believe, if we can buy the building and disaffiliate from the RBL, we are better placed to face the future, with our fate firmly in our own hands.
We currently have branch and club annual accounts which we pay our accountants to prepare. Without a branch that bill is halved. The new club accountants could be less complicated than those demanded by the RBL. A simplified version could be cheaper and easier for members to understand.
Subscription fees would be set by us and the money would go to the club, not RBL Head office. We would have no rent or RBL affiliation fees to pay. I have already spoken to a bank, who will

provide free banking for 2 years as a new business.
There would also be savings in clerical and administration costs. Bizarrely, even our insurance would be cheaper, when not part of a collective policy.
Assuming membership remains the same at 1000 and subscriptions are £10, a conservative estimate has the new club over £20,000 a year better off than at present.
Jerry (bach Thomas said; *"The procedure of disaffiliation is complicating and time consuming, but in his view, the benefits far outweigh the negatives, so we have to create a new club"*
David (grump) Hughes said that he concurred with his fellow officers comments while also making the point;
"There would be no higher authority to blame if things go wrong, no passing the book to the RBL, it will be our club and our responsibility to make sure its successful."
He then moved the motion;
" The Club disaffiliate from the Royal British Legion and agrees to purchase the Kings Head for £110,000 from the RBL"
The motion was carried overwhelmingly.

We found ourselves, back in Pickwick's, angry with the RBL official who was less concerned about the fate of the club, than the windfall the RBL expected when selling the Kings Head.
In the space of a few days, we have decided to disaffiliate, buy the Kings Head building and create a new club. We will have to close the club and branch and complete the annual accounts for each. All this and much more, will need to be done in the next 3 months before the end of September 2013.
This is going to be the most dramatic and frantic few months for the committee. This will test our resolve as officers, taking us into new regulatory and licensing issues, outside our normal expertise. We will have to move incredibly fast, to meet the timeframe agreed with the Estates department of the RBL.

Chapter 42

14 years ago, when we first met, the task ahead was to rescue the club from closure, stabilise its finances, make the branch less dominant and bring in good practices to make the club more accountable to its members.
For my part, there was no confidence we would succeed in any of the goals we set ourselves, being either expelled from the club or overwhelmed by the task in hand.
No one could have predicted back then, how successful the club would become, or the three of us would still be here, facing another unique challenge.
Myself and Jerry were already contemplating retirement from the committee, believing we had fulfilled our function and it was time to make way for some younger charges.
With my 65 birthday coming soon in August 2014, the plan was to see this financial year out, retiring on the last day September, after 15 years service, with a new secretary in place by October 1st, 2014, the start of our club year.

"Events" rarely go to plan, now or in the past as as I recall;
I starting a 5 year apprenticeship in a Coventry factory, 4 months before my 16th birthday, being the youngest of the apprentice intake, after leaving school at Easter, 1964.
After 5 years, while working, now as a craftsman, but still being paid as an apprentice, I demanded the skilled rate, having completed my 5 year apprenticeship.
"No, they said, we will pay you in four months time when your 21 years of age."

The dispute went on for 2 years, with no support from my trade union, before a tribunal found in my favour.
The City Council then made me a *"Freeman of the City of Coventry"* as the youngest ever time-served craftsman.
This entitled me to *"graze my sheep on common land in Coventry and be hung with a silk rope if given a death sentence"*.
David said
"There were times in the last 15 years he would gladly use that silk rope on me and plenty others would enjoy the spectacle".
This was another example of being a " bloody *nuisance*," a few years before Roger Mason first nominated me as a shop steward.
David also took great pleasure in reminding me, He and Jerry were proved right about the club finances, saying;
" Well smart arse, the policy of keeping our capital reserves high, against your opposition, means we can buy the club, without borrowing, no thanks to you Mick Pickwick"
I replied
"We had this policy before we even dreamt about buying the club, and the investment return of £14,000, and the ***£27,000 VAT rebate contributed to the cash reserves"
Jerry and David were having none of this, threatening again to;
"Find a good use for that silk noose, if I did not admit I was wrong on this issue"
I had to concede; *"without the last beer price increase, it would have stretched our resources to buy the Kings Head from the RBL"*
*** Three years later the VAT rebate appeal the government launched was successful, resulting in the club paying £27,000 back over a 4 year period.
The rebate had nonetheless already served its purpose, providing a quarter of the sum needed to buy the Kings Head and negating the need to borrow from the bank or brewery.

> "We're just two lost souls,
> swimming in a fish bowl
> year after year"
> Pink Floyd
> "Wish you were here"

Chapter 43

Not unexpectedly Jerry found a flaw in my retirement plan, pointing out;
"When you have written the new rule book, Mr Secretary and spent the next few months setting up a new club and all the administration involved in that, you can't walk away, 12 months later."
""Why not? The members will own the club, there will be a minimum of £30,000 in the bank, with no loans from the bank or brewery. We will have finished the job we started, with the club in great shape to face the future" I ventured.
Unperturbed Jerry said;
"The first set of accounts for the new club will not be approved by the AGM for another 18 months, taking us to March 2015. We need two years of accounts audited and approved which show the new club is a success, before any of us walk away, that will take us to March 2016.
If we leave before then and it all goes tits up, we will get the blame and have our reputations rubbished in the process"
David fully conferred with this assessment nodding and smiling his approval.
I could not recall agreeing to write a new rule book, or setting up a new company, which is effectively what I have just been saddled with, while having my retirement plan increased to 2016 when I will be 67 years of age.
Experience tells me there will be more and more cunning plans

in the future and the exit door from "*Hotel California*" will remain forever closed.

While the process of buying the club is ongoing there was a mountain of paperwork to get started on. To complicate matters further we decided to upgrade the general manager responsibilities, they will now take on many of the duties previously done by the secretary. The manager would now do VAT and Gaming Machine Duty, work rotas, staff discipline, and wages, under the supervision of the club secretary, on behalf of the club committee.

While these changes were taking place, Stan Roberts was appointed temporary manager for six months.

The club then appointed Sam Jones as general manager, others who have held the role since include Tanya Scheltinga and Llinos Jones.

That position continues today, with Cameron Smith taking office in 2022.

Consulting the members on what the new club should be called during 2013 led to some lively debates, most ex British Legion clubs keep a connection to the military in their title, such as "comrades" or "ex service".

Members were given 3 choices in a ballot for a new name for the club and Jerry's suggestion of using Welsh in the title, found almost universal approval.

Unsurprisingly my "*St Jude's Club for Lost Causes*" never made it onto the ballot paper, but "Clwb Llanrwst Club" gained almost universal approval beating "ex service" and "sports and social" decisively.

There was an overwhelming desire to have a fresh start, with the younger element especially, favouring a less formal structure to that synonymous with the Royal British Legion.

There were still elements adamant the break from the RBL was unnecessary and were unconvinced by the argument we advanced, believing we had an hidden agenda.
The truth is far less "*clandestine*" than people imagine.
"We reacted to circumstances on almost every occasion, whether it was disputes about gaming machines, the women's section, losing our licence, branch resignations or the threat of the club closing. Even the disaffiliation from the RBL was a reaction to the threat of losing possession of the Kings Head building.
Sorry to disappoint, but there was no master plan"

Some people *"just love conspiracy theories"* believing the most bizarre distorted truths, so for those so inclined, this is for you;
David, Jerry and I are part of a fanatical religious cult;
We call ourselves; "*The crazy cult* "
The clues are obvious, the biblical connections easily recognizable by those with sufficient insight.
"*Michael*" is the only Archangel named in the bible.
"He holds the secret of the mighty words" It says.
"*Michael*" has certainly written hundreds of letters, minutes and thousands of words including the current rulebook.
"*David slayed Goliath before becoming a prophet and later King*"
Our "*David*" may not have slayed any giants, but he cracked a few heads together as chairman of the club and was definitely a leader of men.
Jerry's real name is "*Jeremiah*". We are not making that up.
"*Jeremiah*" is the longest book in the bible and he famously said;
"*So my persecutors will stumble and not prevail. They will fail and be thoroughly disgraced; their dishonour will never be forgotten*"
Does this sound familiar, like the dishonourable exit from the dodgy election in the club in 1999..

"*The crazy cult*" have conspired for 15 years with religious zeal to brainwash our members;.
Be careful how you say it, our motto is;
"*Long live the crazy cult*"

There were numerous bodies with regulatory powers, we had to satisfy, prior to setting up a new club. I spoke to other club secretaries who have gone through this process, unfortunately all had used solicitors, paying them thousands of pounds, money they could ill afford. I mentioned this to David, who showed little sympathy telling me;
"Get on with it, were not paying solicitors, remember when they had a policy of not telling us our licence was due, bunch of crooks the lot of them"
I took from that, he expected the secretary to complete the mass of paperwork required including writing a new rule book.
The *"new Rulebook "*, was mostly written while holidaying with Gill in Cromford near Matlock, Derbyshire in September 2013.
It met Conwy Licencing, the Charity Commission and Financial Conduct Authority (FCA) approval after being voted acceptable by the new club committee on my return from a much deserved break.
Big Rich cheekily questioned why;
"*The secretary was taking holidays when we have not finalised the purchase of the club yet*".
The Secretary replied;
"*Given my excessive secretarial club and branch commitments at the moment, notwithstanding the setting up of a new club, with all that entails , Gill and I could not get away during the summer, so any complaints should be taken-up with her.*
Big Rich, not renowned for his diplomacy, displayed good judgement on this occasion, when not taking up this invitation.

By the time we got to October 2013 the start of our financial year, all suppliers, service providers and utilities were aware we were no longer a Royal British Legion. Our bank and others were cutting hours or closing in town so we switched to HSBC. Later they closed, leaving Llanrwst bereft of banks or building societies.

The club later moved to the Coop bank, which provides better and cheaper services for,"not- for- profit/charitable organisations". There is no physical Coop bank, the local post office provides a service on their behalf. Our annual banking fees have reduced by 75%, mainly because we pay far less for depositing and drawing cash from the Coop bank, who we continue to bank with to the present day.

During the process of buying the Kings Head building, the club donated the car park to the British Legion, who subsequently included it in the sale to us. This meant the whole site, building and car park were under the same ownership for the first time since 1968, prior to the sale.

A little later than planned, David, Jerry and I signed the paperwork on Friday 11th October 2013 as we exchanged contracts and purchased the Kings Head, so after nearly half a century, the members finally regained possession of their club, lock, stock and barrel.

Sunday 13th October, we had our last drink in the RBL Llanrwst club. It did not feel like a celebration, we all seemed to be in shock. Seventeen long years since the start of our campaign and the Royal British Legion Club has gone.

Tomorrow, Clwb Llanrwst club comes into existence and gives us a new challenge.

Who knows what lies ahead?

The Llanrwst football team kit sponsored by Clwb Llanrwst Club

Steve Carney, Ken Davies, Jerry Thomas, Gary "Wynn" and Mattie Evans

Chapter 45

The first meeting of Clwb Llanrwst Club was held on Monday evening,14th October 2013 chaired by David Hughes, vice chairman in the absence of Edgar Parry.

Out of nowhere, there was an unexpected outburst of emotion, with everyone on their feet clapping, which continued for a minute or so, but seemed much longer. There were some tears too as years of frustration came to the surface.

Big hard men like David and his brother Richard, not prone to sentimentality, were also caught in the moment. Those tears were not for the loss of the RBL, but a collective relief that we had finally "Crossed the Rubicon" and were ready to start again.

The Secretary reported the club did not pay any legal fees other than £900 conveyancing fees, when purchasing the club and the building was valued at just over £250,000.

Membership fees were set at £10 a year.

With a new computerised membership system, we can for the first time, recruit membership during the whole 90 hours the club is open during the week.

Ken Davis President reminded us of;

"Our promise to; continue with Armistice and the Poppy Appeal" during his submission.

During Ken's talk I suddenly remembered I had missed something out in my opening presentation, so interrupted him. I was quickly reprimanded and put in my place for my rude interjection by Ken. There was an embarrassing silence, before making my apologies.

After the meeting, Ken approached me at the bar, to say he had overreacted. On this point he was wrong, I fully warranted a bollocking. The most senior and highly respected president of the committee deserved better and despite having a drink and a

laugh together afterwards, I still felt guilty.
Not the most auspicious start to a new era of professionalism, competence or harmonious relationships for the new club.

There had been many doom-mongers, predicting a mass exodus of members and a collapse in bar sales following the demise of the RBL club. They have been proved spectacularly wrong, as during the first six weeks 643 members had already joined, including 181 new members. Bar takings were up 15%, coupled with over £6000 in subscriptions (all subscriptions in the past went to the RBL head office) resulting in an improved bank balance of £45,000.
The insurance costs as an independent club have also reduced considerably, after we shopped around for a better deal.
The Brewery, Molson Coors have provided a new sign for the entrance to the club, and talks to reduce the expected brewery increases were successfully concluded.
The chairman said rental costs and RBL affiliations fees are confined to history, saving over £5,000 a year. An improved financial outlook, means that price rises due to take place in January 2014, can now be shelved, should this be the committee's wish.
There was total unanimity with the chairman's assessment.
As an independent club, we wanted sport to take centre stage, whether that is watching or participating, so strengthening ties with Llanrwst's well run football and cricket clubs was high on our agenda.
Over many years the club have contributed towards their facilities and kit. That financial support has increased of late, but it is also money well invested, with the club benefiting from increased sales, as the players choose Llanrwst club as their local watering hole.
You will see many youngsters around town, proudly wearing their

shirts emblazoned with their sponsor "Clwb Llanrwst".
The Football club is well served by Managers and organisers, Chris Williams, David Harold, Mattie Evans, Steven Carney, Gary Wynn and many others too numerous to mention. The same applies to Llanrwst Cricket club, where Maggie Smith, Trevor Williams, Lee Thomas, Aled Hughes, Nathan Jones and Gareth Jones are part of a well run management team. Amazingly Trevor, Lee, Aled and Nathan were playing cricket for Llanrwst 30 years ago, when we first came to town and are still getting padded up, for the team today (2024)

We have very little trouble in the club, with a "*No Tolerance Policy*" in place regarding abuse of staff or fellow members. It is important that the club is seen as a safe place.
It is much more than a place members go for a drink.
For many it's where they see old friends and sadly on some occasions it's where they say goodbye to old friends.
For others it might be the only human contact they have, on a daily basis, especially for those living alone.
For members struggling with energy bills, It can be a warm, friendly space during the winter, whether having a drink or not, it's their space and they will always be welcome.
A young member involved in a minor indiscretion, assumed wrongly he would be suspended, pleading his case for forgiveness to Jerry and David stating;
"*He and his mates love the club, he joined on his 18 birthday and could not bear the thought of ever being excluded*"
This epitomises the popular appeal the new club has, particularly amongst the younger membership, who need to be encouraged and supported, for the club to have future in the long term.

Chapter 46

There was a time when nothing got organised unless senior officers from the club were involved. It has taken a long time, but we have thankfully advanced from that position. Decisions on funding still remain the remit of the committee but wider participation has been encouraged and has come to fruition on many fronts.

Younger committee members are taking on more responsibility. David (Cookie)Williams and Craig Jones administer the pool, which today has 3 teams, when previously, we only had one team for many years. We are heavily involved in the county pool set-up where Ken Davis's grandson Cameron represents the club's interests. A second pool table has been purchased to meet growing demand.

Many years ago the club was approached by county darts players unhappy with the facilities they currently had west of the Llanrwst towards Banger. County administrators visited Llanrwst and were given a presentation on the benefits of relocating, while also offering sponsorship.

Nothing came of it and we found out later our presentation was considered;

"too good to be true" by the administrators and was therefore rejected despite protests from the players.

It was actually a deliverable plan, and if those sceptics visited today, they would see;:

The *"to good to be true"* vision has become a reality.

Darts has gone from a single dartboard, badly positioned in the bar area to five boards in the entertainment room. The club sponsors the league in the president's name,

" The Ken Davies Darts League".

There is increased darts activity, with local and county league participation, tournaments and league presentations at the club. We have also had the former world champion Bob Anderson, complimenting the club on its darts facilities, during his visit.
Kevin Bisp and Ryan Roberts, amongst others, take the plaudits for the administration of the darts which has grown in popularity over the last few years. Jerry and Bobby should also take a bow for installing the boards, oches and lighting, making the club the premier venue for darts in the Conwy Valley.
There is also a "Poker Night", where the players compete against each other, with only limited stakes allowed. Players can join regional and national events, some have qualified and travelled to compete in Las Vegas in the past.
Some years ago poker player Peter Pierce approached the committee about moving to the club, following a breakdown in relations with their former host. The club was happy to accommodate them. There are no officers of the club involved in this activity other than giving them the authority to use the club's facilities.
The club also has sponsorship links with Llanrwst Bowls club.

The committee retired to the bar after the inaugural meeting reflecting on the magnitude of the changes the last six months have brought. Colin Owen said;
"People see the club as theirs now, there's a sense of belonging. We can look to the future, free from the constraints we all experienced from the late 1990s till recently"
The staff and management have all had to rise to the challenge and adapt to an ever changing technological environment. Sheila and Cath's contribution in the office is immeasurable and the committee is forever grateful to them.

> "Don't cry
> don't raise an eye
> It's only teenage wastelands"
> The Who
> "Baba O'Riley"

Chapter 47

In a quiet corner David, Jerry and I disbanded the finance committee, after 15 years, it had run its course. We commented on the fact no minutes were ever taken. The ad hoc meetings were used to hammer out our differences, and find consensus, so we could display a united front to the RBL committees.

Now we are an independent club, our clandestine meetings have become superfluous, as there are no RBL rules to conform to, no senior RBL officers making life difficult and no branch landlords setting the rent.

Our new situation only produced one negative thought. In the past, there was always an element of them and us, when dealing with Royal British Legion officialdom. Our new change of status means;

"There was no one else to blame now, when things go wrong, being masters of our own destiny, brings extra responsibility and accountability for every committee member"

The next time we were sitting in Pickwick's courtyard, there was none of; *"Jerry's cunning plans"* it was a social occasion.

David espoused the; *"failings of the Welsh government, and had solutions to several world conflicts which were far simpler to resolve than those in the club"* in his considered opinion.

The RBL annual accounts were far more complicated than was necessary in our opinion, so the new club needed to change the format. We spoke to our accountant, Andrew Erasmus from Aston Hughes, in Colwyn Bay about simplifying them, given our new status as a private club. He agreed and annual accounts have become less complicated and more relevant to the committee and members now.

The Secretary's role for many years was a time consuming and pressurised job, it's much less so today. It is not by accident, but very much by design this transformation has occurred.

The introduction of a general manager has allowed the committee to concentrate on policy, rather than general governance.

Having no RBL club or branch committees, cuts down on administration as does quarterly, rather than monthly meetings. New technology in bookkeeping, communications, electronic tills and internet services, saved time and expense. Dean Sandham, committee member, had some experience in this field, so advised on the roll out of new technology.

Edgar Parry, chairman, has been a great servant to the club and town in his role as Llanrwst Mayor, but felt he could no longer continue as chairman, or committee member.

The committee thanked him for his chairmanship of the branch and club over many years, while wishing him well for the future.

*Ryan Roberts (top left) and Kevin Bisp (top right)
our darts organisers with some of their teammates.*

Chapter 48

Following Edgar Parry's retirement in 2013, David Hughes was elected chairman and Jerry Thomas, vice chairman, which meant, along with myself (secretary), the original three *"dissidents"* held all three senior officer positions in the club. Ken Davies was elected president and Sheila Thompson reappointed as treasurer.

Since having a triple bypass, in 2007 walking has been my chosen method of keeping fit. With the stunning backdrop of lakes and mountains on my doorstep, it's the ideal environment for thinking through problems, away from the stresses of everyday life.

Interrupting my friend Ken Davies, club president in full flow at our last meeting, had me contemplating my own behaviour. It was too easy to blame the emotional strain of the club's inaugural meeting.

Not prone to introspection, I did however wonder how many other times I presumed my views took precedence over my fellow committee members. The phenomenal successes the club has achieved has been down to teamwork, but sometimes you get it wrong, as I did on this occasion. By displaying some humility and contrition, I hope to restore trust with Ken and my Llanrwst club friends and colleagues before my impending departure from office.

The new club flourished in its first year and continued this success the next year, growing its cash assets to £63,358.

My time in office ended at the 2016 AGM when I said goodbye after 17 years of service first as treasure, followed by 13 years as secretary. The annual accounts of my final year showed a healthy bank balance of £83,575.

Despite Jerry's best efforts to change my mind, the lyrics of

"The Eagles Classic" did not ring true any more;
"*I checked out of Hotel California.*"	"

Resigning my post was difficult, the camaraderie we had was unparalleled in my experience. We have overcome so many obstacles together as a team, avoided the odd catastrophe and smiled in the face of adversity.

My lasting memory will be the positivity we created, which was in complete contrast to the situation we inherited, but all good things come to an end.

Having a clean break is also essential, as the new secretary needs the space to flourish without the ex- secretary acting as a backseat driver.

Ken Jenkins who previously served as a secretary, when the club was still a Royal British Legion, agreed to fill the vacant secretary position, while also continuing as the Poppy organiser for the RBL. Having worked as treasurer for 4 years with Ken as secretary from 1999, we all knew Ken has all the necessary skills to fulfil the role and is popular amongst the committee, staff and wider membership.

The committee under Ken, David and Jerry's management will ensure the club goes from strength to strength with their experienced hands on the tiller.

We did not know that dark days were ahead.

David Hughes rang me one evening to inform me he had terminal cancer. I have no recollection of that conversation, other than my failings to offer suitable words of comfort to David on behalf of Gill and myself.

How unfair was this, not yet 60 years old, so close to his brother Richard, loved by his partner Sheila and his two sons Jonathan and Christopher, his grandchildren and wider family.

Jerry, while not family loved him like a brother too. Hardly a day goes by when they were not together repairing, or installing things in the club, taking the piss out of each other incessantly. Like David's family, he was also devastated.

If this was not catastrophic enough, not too long afterwards his brother Richard received a similar diagnosis. This horrible disease had taken his wife Gwyneth, who died of cancer in 2004 following the death of her son Dion, in a road accident the year before.

Richard had only just reached retirement age.

The Brothers have been an integral part of our lives, for many years as we worked together for a common cause. That special bond we had, was built on mutual respect, and was the foundation for every successful campaign we took part in.

I recall Big Rich on one occasion helping our club doorman, Cyril with security during Llanrwst show night, when its members only.

Non members will try every trick in the book, to gain entry into the club;

"Can I just pop in to give my sister a message".

"I left my coat last night, can I just go and fetch it?"

They have heard them all before and the answer is always "no".

Someone asks; "Let me in I'm desperate, I need the shithouse"

Richard replies; " You've just found one, now Fxxx off"

Both David and Richard still used the club when well enough between their treatments. They both attended committee meetings, when they could and the "gallows humour" both displayed in adversity was heart wrenching at times.

For many years the front of the club building was in a disgraceful state of repair. It needed £45,000 spending on it to achieve a complete transformation. Discussing future projects would lead to comments like;

"Why are you asking me, I won't be here to see it" or

" Stop rabbiting on about it, you lot will be the death of me.

Agreement was reached to;
"*Stop rabbiting on about the renovation and get on with it ASAP*" with Jerry project managing the operation.
He prepared drawings for the front of the building. The Conwy planning department had other ideas and a prolonged process began. If planning was not bad enough, later Covid would intervene to lengthen this process even further as planners worked from home.

Clwb Llanrwst after the front renovation was completed, within budget, is no longer an eyesore.
It was a project managed by Chairman Jerry Thomas, who dedicated it to David and Richard Hughes.

David and Richard in happier times with brother John and sisters Vanda and Margaret (centre) at a family get together

David clowning about    *David giving Dave(cookie) advice*

Chapter 49

On September 3rd, 2017, Richard died.

A packed church listened to Jerry do the eulogy for our friend, before we all went back to the club to reminisce and exchange stories about his life.

Richard was a larger than life character with a smile that could light up any room, he is a huge loss. He was really popular with everyone at work and in the club. Richard's modesty, undervalued the important role he played in the clubs renaissance.

Big Rich's unwavering support was a source of inspiration to all the club's officers and committee members, who were privileged to stand alongside him.

He had a wicked sense of humour and had a put down for anyone getting ahead of themselves.

"*Go and do one*" was a common refrain if someone overstayed their welcome or tested his patience, but he was never intimidating, despite his size.

David and Richard were not only brothers but best friends, so how David is going to cope with this loss, while so ill himself is a worry for all of us..

As we say goodbye to Big Rich I am comforted by something David grump once said, after I was being mercilessly lambasted by Big Rich;

"Don't worry Mick, Big Rich saves his best insults for his friends". That thought has stayed with me forever, that comment reveals as much about David as it does about Richard.

I feel honoured that Richard considered me his friend.

Before retiring from the committee, many of us wanted the club to be a "*go to venue*" for live music in the Conwy Valley. A few attempts to achieve this failed and it was time to have another

look at it. Mike Marsh and Geraint Jones said that we need to invest in a sound system and technical equipment.
Mike knows everyone on the music scene and hosts these events with great humour. Sound engineering is Geraint's forte having worked with many artists. Both have good contacts and were confident that upgrading the system would work.
David on hearing how much was going to cost, got into his usual tirade, claiming;
"Ken Jenkins and Jerry Thomas are as bad as the last secretary Mick Pickwick at wasting money on frivolous projects".
David had the whole committee believing he was against this, before breaking into a smile. That sense of humour never left him. Now that the investment has come to fruition, musicians have nothing but praise for the growing reputation of Llanrwst Clwb as a music venue. The *"open mic night"* held once a month in the club draws in a lot of local musical talent and is always well attended.
(*Mike Marsh in 2024 informed us that Parkinson's Disease has robbed him of his ability to play guitar and act as MC on open mic nights. Mike loves his music, life can be such a cruel bastard at times.*)

Jerry had been a regular visitor to see David, while he was being treated at home. My visits were less frequent but in mid September 2018 Jerry and I arranged to take David out for the day. Sheila, his partner, a former nurse, reminded us before we left, that it was David's wish to be DNR (Do Not Resuscitate) should his condition worsen.
David wanted to visit the lakes Crafnant and Gerionedd above Trefriw, where unknown to me, he had lived for a time.
Passing through Trefriw, we passed an old man with a stick, he looked about 90 years old.
David said;

"That old farmer is a right bastard, never paid me for working on his house, you should run him over"

A little further on he said;

"Stop, I put that roof on that house, miserable pair of sods they were, tight arses too".

He further recalled that one neighbour had half a dozen lawn mowers and when David's mower packed up, he asked;

"If he could borrow one, till the new one he ordered arrived."

What David called him when he refused, could not be spoken in polite company and could lead to a court proceedings if repeated in public.;

Reliving these stories, was David Grump at its finest.

It was a memorable drive, on a beautiful sunny day, he was in his finest *"grump mode"* in the car and at the lakeside cafe, complained how much the ice creams were, insisting;

"Tight arse Pickwick puts his hand in his pocket for a change to buy them and I'll buy them next time"

Jerry and I still talk about that last day the three of us spent together and remember how he never lost that infectious, insatiable sense of humour or courage during his final days.

We agreed to meet again a week later on September 28th and go out for a drive again. On reaching David's house, we saw there many cars, close by and nowhere to park.

It was plain to us the family had gathered, so not wishing to intrude, we left, only to learn soon afterwards, tragically David had died.

At the funeral Jerry gave a fine eulogy in the church, before we went to Clwb Llanrwst for the funeral buffet.

There's a corner of the bar Richard and David used to occupy, with a photograph of them looking down. We gathered there under their gaze, finding it hard to believe they were no longer with us.

Looking back to our first courtyard encounter in 1996, it is very clear there would be *"no dissidents"* without David.

At key moments David seized the initiative, taking the gratuities book, to stop free drinks being handed out, setting the tone for future reforms. He further confiscated the bandit keys from the branch, which allowed the club to receive the income from the gaming machine, giving a two word reply,when the branch wanted compensation.

"Does that help with the cash flow problem, Mr treasurer?"

He memorably said to me afterwards, with a wide grin on his face

These were crucial interventions when the club had no money, best summed up by the Llanrwst bank manager at the time;

"The club is not an economic proposition"

David's summary of the situation was more down to earth and one the average member can easily relate too;

"The club has been abandoned by the British Legion, membership figures are shit, it's up to its arse in debt to the brewery and a basket case to the bank"

David recruited Jerry Thomas and myself as fellow *"dissidents"* in a madcap desperate attempt to save the club from imminent closure, completely ignoring the fact this foolhardy mission had little prospect of success.

Often taken for granted, this much loved club is an essential part of Llanrwst's social fabric. It's no exaggeration to say without David's iron resolve, this community asset would have been lost forever.

That's David's legacy, his lasting legacy.

The Llanrwst town and club have lost two of their finest in David and Richard Hughes;,

"The likes of which, we will never see again"

"REST IN PEACE MY FRIENDS".

Richard and David Hughes

This photo of *"Big Rich and Dave "Grump"*
is above the corner of the bar,
where they once gathered with a group
of like minded "dissidents".
They sadly are no longer with us ,
but make no mistake they are
looking down on us, making sure
the standards they enshrined
are maintained in their absence.

> *"You can't always get what want,*
> *but if you try sometimes,*
> *well you just might find*
> *you get what you need"*
> Rolling Stones.
> *"You can't always get what you want"*

Chapter 50

Jerry's unenviable task of redeveloping the front of the club, replacing the existing eyesore, was proving more difficult than expected. The club has a policy of using local labour, wherever possible, preferably members of the club, which was the case during this project.. Planning decisions had delayed the start before Covid intervened, making decision making even more difficult as council employees worked from home.

Four years of frustration, before work could commence and finally Jerry had something to *"project manage"*. Local tradesmen Stuart Davis and Chris Parry eventually started the restoration of the front elevation of the club after the Davis Brothers, another local firm, had erected the scaffolding.

Neil Thomas, a local businessman fitted the windows. Neil, a lifelong member of the club, who at a later date, also joined the club committee. Today, Jerry and Neil are ever present in the club carrying out repairs, doing all those essential behind the scene jobs

They have recently (2024) with the help of Colin Owen and Wayne Hughes installed a roof lantern in the main bar to improve ventilation and introduce some natural light to the room. Local painter Gareth Towers added the final touches to this long overdue improvement.

Cath Evans bookkeeper, decided to retire, she is the last link to a time before the reforms in the late 1990s. Sheila Thompson also retired as treasurer.

When cash was king, prior to Covid, Cath and Sheila literally counted millions in coins over the years, before depositing them in the local bank. They also along with Ken Jenkins counted and banked the contents of the poppy appeal boxes for more than 20 years.

Very few people are aware of the roles these two women fulfilled, being out of sight in our offices above the club entrance. Myself and fellow officers however, do acknowledge and fully appreciate the role they played in making the club the success it is today.

There were some particularly testing times for the club when Barclays bank denied us access to our business account for months and Covid also threw up some unique challenges.

During Covid the club was closed at times, mainly due to staff testing positive and having to isolate at home. More often than not, the club operated on restricted hours, while introducing a waitress service, to conform with social distancing.

With government support and county council grants, the club came through almost unscathed, thanks mainly to Ken Jenkins (secretary), and his staff.

Towards the end of 2023, Cath, 92 years young, was getting into her car to drive home from the local Coop, when our paths crossed. She has now sadly lost Moldwyn her husband, a former doorman in the club, but in hers words "*still ploughs on*".

Sheila, with her sister in law Vanda Hughes, along with Miriam Llewelyn, Ellis Hughes and Helen Pen Parc organise and run the Bingo 2 nights a week on behalf of the committee.

This is another example of members being encouraged to take control of their own activities similar to darts, pool and poker.

Ken Jenkins like David and Richard was also diagnosed with cancer, but bravely continued to carry out his secretarial duties

where possible, with Cameron Smith assisting him with poppy organiser duties with a view to taking over that role in the future. Ken succumbed to the disease in April 2021.
Covid rules meant that only 15 people could attend his funeral, including Jerry who did the eulogy. With the limitation on numbers, many family, friends and colleagues in the club were unable to pay their last respects to Ken.
Sadly, Beryl, his wife also passed away early in 2024.
Ken had been a successful businessman in Llanrwst, never afraid of hard work, often getting up in the middle of the night to drive to Liverpool to buy stock for his greengrocer business and also ran a taxi firm at one time.
He was also a publican in the past, and he utilised that experience to the benefit of the club. First and foremost though, Ken was a real gentleman and a team player. He will be remembered fondly by everyone who new him and worked with him

The club now finds itself without a secretary in 2021, following Ken's death. I had no desire to replace Ken again, having first taken over from him as secretary in 2003 after his resignation. I was still using the club, and could not be happier, enjoying the social life, without the burden of office.
Finding time for voluntary ambulance driving for the NHS was a bucket list activity ticked off, in the last few years and I was currently training to do a 3000 miles walk over 333 days, which encompassed Hadrian's Wall, the North Wales coastal footpath and Llyn Peninsula.
Gill and I were also looking to retire from Pickwick's, which was now for sale, so a life of leisure beckoned, with us both fit enough to enjoy the experience.(We sold Pickwick's and retired to Trefriw (2 miles from Llanrwst) in March 2022)

> "The road is long, with many a winding turn,
> That leads us to who knows where,
> Who knows where."
> The Hollies
> "He ain't heavy, he's my brother"

Chapter 51

It will come as no surprise that Jerry Thomas had other ideas, when it came to my plans; *"for a life of leisure"*.
No candidate had come forward to fill the void left by Ken. There is a legal requirement to have a Club secretary, the position is the equivalent of a landlord in a public house. Jerry had tried without success to recruit me again, as the secretary. Persistent as ever, he suggested a compromise, whereby a temporary position is created.
"Just come on board Mick for another year, then we can both retire, I will be 75 years old then" Jerry said.
Ken Davies the club president joined Jerry and waylaid me in a charm offensive at the bar.
I agreed to;
"reconsider my original blanket refusal over the next few days"
The next day I was receiving *"handshakes"* and *"back slapping"* from well wishers for returning to the fold as secretary, despite the fact, I had not actually arrived at a decision yet.
Protesting to Ken and Jerry proved pointless, I had been outflanked yet again, they had even arranged a meeting with the brewery representative, promising my participation that very day, which of course I attended being introduced as the new secretary.
Another cunning plan from Jerry has me;
"Once more into the fray, into the last good fight" (Shakespear)
The club Sponsored my 3000 mile walk, which in total raised

£1500 for a good cause, finishing for good measure with a welcoming ceremony at the club.

The committee agreed to upgrade the men's toilet, which required a complete overhaul. Also during 2021 and 2022 work was progressing on the front of the building under Jerry's project management.. He seems to have acquired an assistant, because almost every day Dave Mark Williams (Mennigs) took on the role as general factotum, unpaid, helping in many ways, come rain or shine.
At the October 2022 club committee meeting, we were able to report the renovation of the building was completed within budget and the gents toilets were also finished to a high standard, both using exclusively local labour.
Town councillors, local business leaders and townsfolk generally welcomed the massive improvement in the club's appearance. Approaching the club from the Betws y Coed direction, the club now stands proud and imposing, replacing the *"eye-saw"* which blighted the centre of town's appearance.
The "*King Head*" restored to its former glory is now a credit to the town for locals and visitors alike. The members can be proud they contributed their hard earned cash to make this possible.
Annual General Meetings (AGM's) usual role is to consider the committee's past work, while examining annual accounts from the previous year.
Having approved the annual accounts the AGM deviating from its usual remit, agreeing the;
*Renovation was amongst the club's finest achievements"
of the last few decades along with;*
"Bringing financial stability to the club in the late 1990's".
"Becoming a multi award winning club".
"Purchasing the Kings Head"
"Creating Clwb Llanrwst Club in 2013"..

Chapter 52

During the early part of 2022 Ken Davies, our club president died after a short illness, Ken (number 10) Davies lived at 10 Cae Tyddyn, Llanrwst. He was in many people's eyes, Mr Llanrwst a British Legion legend and club man, through and through.

Ken sadly had lost his wife Dorothy almost 30 years before, everyone remarked what a great couple they were. Ken was at our shoulder for all the battles the "dissidents" fought in the club. He never shied away from any confrontation as our president, and had the total respect from members and fellow officers. There were times when challenges seemed insurmountable and morale was low, never more so, than at the infamous ballot declaration when *"the dissidents"* lost every seat, in a rigged election.

Ken, ever the eternal optimist, refused to be crestfallen.
"Pack up your troubles in your old kit bag and smile, smile, smile". He sang and hummed in total defiance, lifting the mood of everyone.

Ken may have thought himself as a foot soldier, but Jerry was right when he said: *"Ken is the glue that kept us together"*
When others wavered, he stood firm, we could not have had a better team player or finer president than Ken Davies.

Strangely I look back on the *"bollocking"* Ken gave me, as a fond memory, despite my embarrassment at the time.

Ken would also be proud, his son Gary Michael has taken over the presidency of the committee from his father.

Bobby Dean, affectionately known as "little Bobby" who was slightly older than Ken Davies, also died a little later in 2023, both were in their eighties. Bobby may have been diminutive in stature but he was big hearted, hugely popular and much loved

in the club. He always had a smile on his face and displayed an enthusiasm for work and life , which was an example to us all..
He knew every inch of the club, having been the resident electrician for many years and committee member before our involvement, during difficult times for the club. Coming from Liverpool and being a shop steward on large construction sites before moving to Llanrwst, was a tough assignment.
By his own volition he was forthright and bolshie, a real *"old school"* workers representative.
One day whilst recalling a confrontation with an employer, he became extremely agitated, wagging his finger at me, reliving this event from the past. To the casual observer we were having a blazing row and people thought he was really angry with me. He wasn't of course, it was just Bobby's enthusiasm, something that never wavered, like his support for the club, which never faltered.
Random women used to come and hug him at the bar, sometimes his head would disappear into a matronly bosom, before he would eventually emerge, smiling, glasses steaming, as he came up for air.
Lovely man, complete one off and like Ken Davies will never be forgotten..
A bench dedicated to Ken Davis, Standard bearer and Ken Jenkins Poppy organiser, now has pride of place by the Cenotaph, donated by the club committee.

From time to time we extend the democratic franchise to consult the whole membership, as happened when choosing the club's new name in 2013.
In 2023 The committee debated whether to increase subscriptions which had remained at £10 for 10 years since becoming an independent club. It was decided to ballot our 1000 members with 3 options.

1. Subscriptions £20 with no increase in prices.
2. Subscriptions £15 with 10p a pint increase
3. Subscriptions £10 with 20p a pint increase.
1 All outcomes were equally acceptable to the committee.
The price freeze "*option 1*" would last a year and be reviewed in October 2024.
The debate about the merits of each proposal was heated at times, but the regulars soon worked out they were "*quids in*" with option 1, which was favoured by an 80% majority in a secret ballot.
This decision meant the 2019 pre-Covid price of £2.50 for the clubs best selling lager had remained unchanged for 5 years.

Just before going to print in late October 2024 the committee agreed to increase beer prices by 30p a pint. We live in an uncertain world, but providing nothing untowards happens, there will be no further increases before the next review in October 2026.

Poster for the charity walk sponsored by Clwb Llanrwst

Clwb Llanrwst Club
23 Nov 2021

3000 MILE FUND RAISING WALK

Mick Bucknall, Clwb secretary will complete the 333-day walk finishing at Clwb Llanrwst on
Sunday 28th November at 4pm
He is fund raising for Tia Howard, age 11 who has a rare form of cancer.
Donations can be made on Mick's Facebook (just giving), at the bar or to the door person.

Chapter 53

I have now celebrated my 75th birthday (2024),10 years on from my original retirement plan and 3 long years have passed since my temporary (*12 month*) appointment in March 2021.
My replacement as secretary has still not materialised, which will come as no surprise to anyone, especially Jerry Thomas.
Jerry is now 78 years old, and still continues as chairman, despite exceeding his own retirement plan by 5 years or more.
You wonder if those *"pearly gates"* might come into focus for Jerry and I, while still in office, unless younger people *"step up to the plate"* sooner rather than later..
Cameron Smith has grown into the role as general manager, having been in the post now for over 2 years. We have developed a good working relationship and without tempting fate seem to have avoided the presence of;
"St Jude the patron saint of hope and lost causes" during his tenure to date

There is a gap in our knowledge regarding the history of the Kings Head, which we were keen to examine further.
It became clear during the renovation that parts of the building dated back over 400 years, yet we have no records beyond the 1890's.
Jerry, Neil Thomas travelled to the Caernarfon records office to garner more information from the archives.
It was a very fruitful expedition and we now have copies of the original deeds from 1815, that trace the ownership and tenancies, from then to the present day.
This proves beyond doubt the building has been called the Kings Head for over 200 years, as it was purchased with that title. It is highly probable it is the original name of the building, unless it predates *"the reformation"*.

The 1886 Indenture and 1825 Deeds.

Now framed and on permanent display in the club lounge. The annual rent charged in 1886 was £250 a year, This seems high for the time, but there were stabling and outhouses on the site that exists today. The new owners purchased the building for £1,300 with a mortgage.

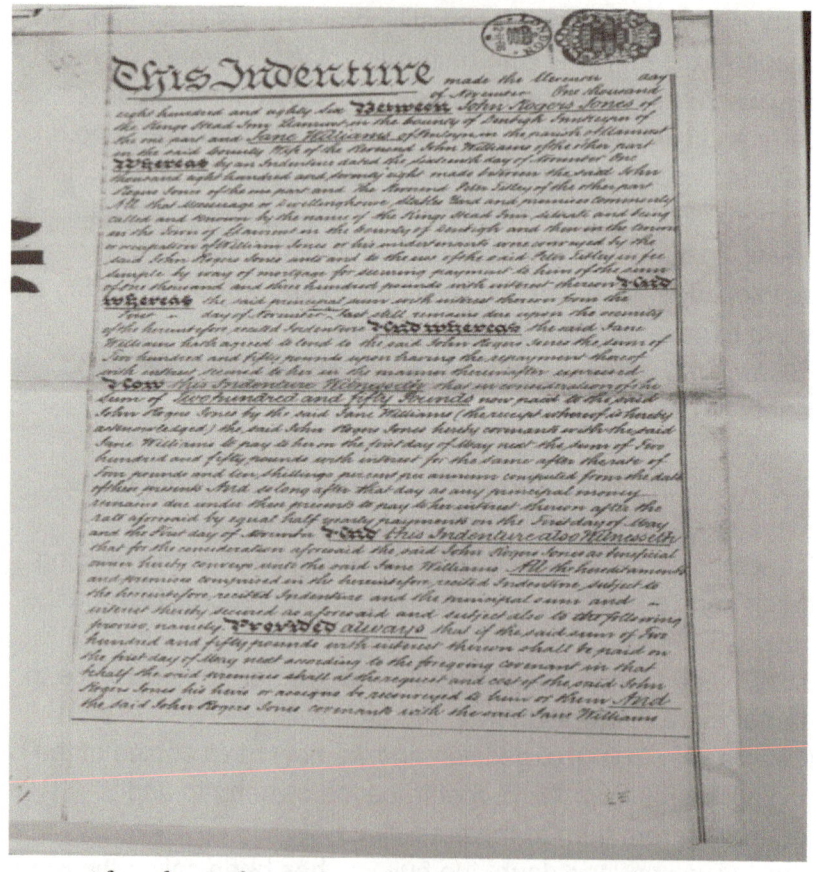

After the Reformation, Henry V111 in 1534 split from the Catholic Church. At that time "*Pope's Head*" inns were widespread, but were forced to change their name and "The *Kings Head*" came into common usage.

Peter Robert Burrell-Drummond of Drummond Castle Perth, MP for Boston, Lincolnshire purchased the King Head with a multitude of outbuildings paying £910 for the property in 1815. It was leased to John Williams, Llanrwst innkeeper with John Griffiths, Llanrwst, listed occupation, Gentleman named in the title deed.

In 1820 on the death of his father, Peter Burrell-Drummond now Baron Gwydyr, succeeded his father and was ennobled into the House of Lords.

There are coloured etchings of his lordship by artist Richard Dighton from 1818 showing him in all his pomp, described as a *"great dandy"* of his day, who enjoyed the delights of Paris.

Mrs Clementina Drummond- Burrell seems a much more interesting character being an active member of high society often referred to as "the Infamous" Mrs Drummond Burrell and noted for her lavish parties and excesses. She is captured on canvas on many occasions by the court painters of the day.

An Haven of Sobriety

We can also now confirm from the Deeds, that *"The Kings Head"* was the home of the Temperance Society , serving nothing stronger than tea just over a century ago.

Also in our possession is a poster advertising the *"Kings Head Temperance Hotel"*, which existed for a decade at the start of the 20th century.

The new owners of the Kings Head Llanrwst in 1820 following the death of Baron Gwydyr

Sir Peter Robert Drummond- Burrell   Lady Clementina
1782 -1865   1809- 1882
Source... David William Wilkins Weblog.

Clementina was the only surviving child of James Drummond the 11th Earl of Perth who married Sir Peter in 1807. In 1814 she was the youngest of a group of Patronesses of Almacks. There were several dances named after her. Her father died in 1800 leaving her a large fortune. They took the name Drummond as their family name at the insistence of Clementina as part of the agreed marriage settlement. She was considered a "stickler" and "overly grand" and was visited at their home Castle Drummond in 1842, by Queen Victoria.

The Patronesses of Almack's: The Arbiters of London Respectability

Almack's Assembly Rooms was governed by a select committee of the most influential and exclusive ladies of the ton, known as the Lady Patronesses of Almacks.

Lest we Forget

The bench was installed by the Llanrwst Cenotaph in 2024. Dedicated to Ken Davies who served the RBL as a Standard Bearer, Poppy seller and Club President and Ken Jenkins Poppy Organiser for the RBL and RBL Club Secretary, and later Clwb Llanrwst Secretary. Both served with distinction and will always be remembered fondly.

The Bench was Donated by The Clwb Llanrwst Club Social fund.

The Club gave a commitment in 2013 it would continue to provide a Poppy organiser and pay for a Buffet in the club each Armistice. We are pleased to say, we have kept that promise. The Bench is a thank you, to the two Kens and all those who lost their lives for us since 1914.

Chapter 54

There is reference earlier in the book, to a conversation one Christmas, being like a script from Monty Python's Flying Circus, which Big Rich succinctly called ;"talking shite"
Well Rich if you're looking down on us, here's another one..

The Chairman's Chair. A Modern Fairytale.
Once upon a time there were half a dozen chairs at the bar in the middle room of Llanrwst Club. We know they are stools really, but HR (Human Resources) advised us to avoid the word "*stools*" because of their Lavatoral connection.
Five chairs have now succumbed to the riggers of everyday life and are sadly no more.
The one remaining rickety chair is old, disfigured and well past its usefulness. This inanimate object, has had a tough time over the years, being subjected to daily misuse, as were its former wooden companions, prior to being skipped .
The last chair's seat has absorbed gallons of alcohol, not to mention other embarrassing leakages and daily bouts of flatulence during its miserable existence..
The only friends this lonely chair had were Dave and Jerry, who lovingly refurbished this beleaguered chair, before inexplicably forming a genuine affection for this much maligned object.
Following renovation, the Chairman David Grump relocated this chair to the corner of the bar, where it seemed happier and where it still remains today.
From that day forth, this was no longer just a chair, this became The "*Chairman's Chair*" and a true partnership was born..
The "*Chairman's Chair*" now assumed greater status, seating Chairman David as he held court surrounded by colleagues and friends.
When the Chairman was not in attendance, the Chairman's Chair

was allowed to rest from its labours. Anyone sitting in the Chairman's chair quickly vacated it, when its rightful incumbent Chairman David made an appearance.

When Jerry took over the Chairmanship, he quickly formed a similar bond with the Chairman's Chair and you will see them most evenings enjoying each other's company.

We trust their partnership will long lasting and they both:
"Live happily ever after" ……….. *The End*

Human Resources……Warning:
Should any reader(s) be of a sensitive nature and find themselves traumatised by the ill treatment of inanimate objects in this story, we have a team of trained counsellors waiting to assist you. Please contact the;
Support Helpline Internal Taskforce; "SHIT" for short.

NB; Yes, there really is a Chairman's Chair and it is a stool, as you can clearly see. It is the last surviving chair, rescued by Chairman David Hughes and adopted as his own.
The picture below is the lower torso of the current Chairman, Jerry Thomas sitting on the Chairman's Chair, in the far corner of the bar in the exact spot, his predecessor sat.

> *"And when the broken hearted people*
> *living in the world agree,*
> *there will be an answer*
> *let it be"*
> The Beatles
> *"Let it be"*

Chapter 55

Jerry Thomas chairman strongly believes in *"fate"* and *"Things happen for a reason"*
Our meeting, when Gill and I first came to view a property in Llanrwst was therefore pre-ordained if *"fate"* is to be believed. Everything I did before as a trade union official, according to Jerry's synopsis, was therefore, a preparation for the events of the last 30 years.
Whether it was *"fate"* or more likely coincidence;
"something brought us together"
That *"something"* has taken up almost half of our collective adult lives, remarkably.
Things however could have turned out so differently, without a bit of luck on my part or did *"fate"* intervene.

On the 12th October 1984, I was part of a delegation assembled at Esher College, London to travel to The Grand Hotel Brighton to lobby the Minister of Defence, Procurement Minister Alan Butler, (*working under Michael Heseltine Secretary of State for Defence*). We were there on behalf of the Aerospace Industry trying to persuade the ministry of defence to place orders,to try to save jobs. Our Security passes failed to arrive, so our evening meeting at the Grand Hotel was cancelled. That night the IRA planted a bomb at the Grand Hotel and 5 people lost their lives.The MP Sir Antony Berry was among them.

A close shave for our delegation and in a perverse way, an opportunity for someone else. The by-election resulting from the MPs death, led to Michael Portillo winning the vacant seat. He subsequently introduced the "Poll Tax" in Scotland, which cost him his seat at the next election and eventually led to the downfall of Margert Thatcher.

On the 6th March 1987 "*The Herald of Free Enterprise Disaster*" happened killing 193 people. The year before, some trade union officer colleagues and I took 1000 retired Electrician Union members on that ship for a day out in France. We tried to book the same Ferry in early March the next year, but the Sun newspaper did a voucher promotion for its readers, giving them a free trip, which filled the whole Ferry. So we had to make other arrangements
We booked the sister ship,"*The Spirit of Free Enterprise*" instead a week or so earlier and had a wonderful time.
We could only look on, in horror as the events at Zeebrugge when the ferry capsized, knowing that could easily have been us.

So while Jerry and I can agree to differ, over whether fate intervened or not, in our long association at Llanrwst club, we can agree with absolute certainty on one thing;
"*That failing business, formerly the Llanrwst Royal British Legion club, later renamed Clwb Llanrwst Club has been transformed from a loss making venture, on the brink of closure, into a successful multi award winning club, with a turnover of half a million pounds today*"

Can you decide if "fate" played a part?

The End

Appendix

So why write a book and why now, you might ask?
 If your conversation with your wife invariably ends with;
"I told you that yesterday , don't you remember" or worse, your grandchildren raise their eyebrows, giving the impression;
"your losing it", It really is time to take stock.
Selective amnesia has been a trusted friend for years, but if my continued cantankerousness moves further towards cognitive decline, it's now or never journalistically for me.
This publication is primarily written as a homage to my friends and colleagues, whose achievements otherwise, may be forgotten and get
" lost in the mists of time"
 After almost 30 years, I also feel qualified to offer our eventual successors a piece of advice.
That is remember *"officialdom"* is not there to help you.
Whether it be bankers, council officials, planners, lawyers or other bureaucrats, they all have an aversion towards the concept called *"change".*
Detractors will argue your ambitions should be constrained, so don't settle for mediocrity, because there is only one question which counts, after your time in office ceases.
"Have you left the club in a better state, than the one you inherited?"
In our case, I think most people would answer that question with a *"yes"* and hopefully our successors will be able to say the same.
"We wish them well"

Finding a title for this book was far from straightforward;
(a) *"Not an Economic Proposition"*
Reminds us what the clubs bankers thought of the clubs prospects and was a real contender.
(b) *"The Rise of the Dissidents"*, was a working title at one time.
(c) In the end though the *"say-it-as-it-is"* from Big Rich's *got the nod*, with his *"f"* word left out, although it might attract more readers, left in.
"Over a Fxxxxxx Barrel, 30 year of Llanrwst club"

This *"Winston Churchill"* quote equally applies to me now;
"History will be kind to me, because I intend to write it"
So you should read my version of the club's history, with the above caveat in mind.
This is not a definitive record, there is no such thing. This is my account and it's obviously highly subjective. It would be totally different, if told from the perspective of some former committee members and employees prior to our time in office.
Their version of events would cast David and Jerry as villains with me, the "*devil incarnate*" no doubt.
Even today, sadly, a limited number of people hold us in such disregard, even contempt, they have not spoken to my colleagues or me, or set foot in the club for decades, so deep rooted is their antagonism towards us
Despite our differences in the past, we extend an olive branch to these disaffected ex-members to join the club and put our differences behind us, so we can work together for the good of the club and the wider Llanrwst community.
"*We can all agree to disagree and hopefully move on*".

I first thought about writing this book after David and Richard Hughes died, having already collated a limited history about the Kings Head and the club over the years. Then in 2023, I started the book in earnest, but unfortunately the result was disappointing, being more like a diary, with a set of reports and minutes, with the most important elements,*"the people"*, secondary rather than central to the narrative.
In 2024 another attempt, but this time the ambition was to make the participants real flesh and blood and try to show how important our lasting friendship and sense of humour defined our working relationships.
There have been many setbacks over the years, but I hope the story doesn't come across as a perpetual struggle, because our hard fought successes far exceed the occasional failures. I have had enormous pleasure and made lifetime friends from my long association with the club, and will carry fantastic memories with me into my twilight years.
It's a fine balancing act, being a member, senior officer and employer whilst still trying to be; *"one of the boys"*.
Jerry fulfils this role seamlessly, me less so, but a recent discussion

gives me hope.
Mulling over our legacy one day with some barroom philosophers.
It was noted we already had a Chairman's chair for Jerry, a Hughes brothers corner and a Memorial bench for the two Kens.
"*Where's your lasting legacy mick?*"
They said, "*you have pissed off a lot of people and had to deal with a lot of shit, so you deserve to be remembered Mick*"
Big Rich a master at keeping you grounded, would have approved of their plan to honour my contribution with the;
"*Mick Pickwick Gents toilet*"
A telling testament to my unique talent obviously.

The original "three dissidents" Jerry, David and I were not "Generals" as Ken Davies referred to us, neither were we a "*bunch of pussies*" as professed by Big Rich.
No, we were just ;
"Three ordinary guys doing their best".

It's winter 2024, Jerry is still chairman, with the same enthusiasm   as someone half his age. For my sins and "*Jerry's cunning*" I continue as Club Secretary, in my second term of a 12 month temporary appointment, now in its fourth year.
Everytime I consider retirement, a tune comes into my head ,an annoying "*ear-worm*" that haunts me;

*"You can check out any time you like,
but you can never leave"*

Hotel California.   The Eagles

Acknowledgments

Ianni Robaitsh who read the first draft and encouraged me to publish the book.
Brian Phillips an old mate from Bedworth who introduced me to the concept of self publishing a book.
Daniel Casey, fellow Llanrwst writer, gave me guidance and support.
Grandchildren Chloe Jones, Ben Collimore and son Nathan for their technical support.
Jerry Thomas for his recall of events and people.
Gill Bucknall's grammatical corrections, which were numerous.
Grandchildren Finn Collimore and Lucy Jones for cover design.
Molson Coors financial contribution towards the book.
Thanks to the North Wales Weekly News for the use of their articles.
Big thank you to the Archive and Records office Caernarfon.
Thanks to the Club Mirror awards panel.
Special mention for Dianne Williams Architect. The front Renovation would still be in planning without her intervention.

Lastly thanks to all the staff and committee members who have been part of team "Clwb Llanrwst" and the "Royal British Legion club and branch" during the last three decades.